# TARGET
# NORTH
# KOREA

**Gavan McCormack** is a professor in the Research School of Pacific and Asian Studies at the Australian National University and currently visiting professor at International Christian University in Tokyo. He is author of many studies of East Asian history and politics and his work is widely translated and read in Japanese, Korean and Chinese.

# TARGET

# NORTH
# KOREA

## PUSHING NORTH KOREA TO THE BRINK
## OF NUCLEAR CATASTROPHE

GAVAN MCCORMACK

NATION BOOKS
NEW YORK

TARGET NORTH KOREA: *Pushing North Korea to the Brink of Nuclear Catastrophe*

Copyright © 2004 Gavan McCormack

Published by
Nation Books
An Imprint of Avalon Publishing Group
245 West 17th St., 11th Floor
New York, NY 10011

Nation Books is a co-publishing venture of the Nation Institute and Avalon Publishing Group Incorporated.

Library of Congress Cataloging-in-Publication Data is available.

ISBN 1-56025-557-9

9 8 7 6 5 4 3 2 1

Book design by Paul Paddock
Printed in the United States of America
Distributed by Publishers Group West

# CONTENTS

1 I
THE WORLD'S MOST DANGEROUS REGIME

15 II
THE WAR THAT WAS, 1950-1953

51 III
THE <u>JUCHE</u> WORLD: FATHER, SON, AND STATE

79 IV
THE <u>JUCHE</u> WORLD: GROWTH TO COLLAPSE

101 V
THE KOREAS: ONE PLUS ONE EQUALS ONE

121 VI
JAPAN AND NORTH KOREA: DIFFICULT NEIGHBORS

149 VII
NUCLEAR CHICKEN: THE CONFRONTATION BETWEEN NORTH
KOREA AND THE UNITED STATES

181 VIII
WAR OR PEACE?

199 NOTES

# THE WORLD'S MOST DANGEROUS REGIME

With which country in its more than two centuries of history has the United States been longest at loggerheads? Some might think of George III's England, Hitler's Germany, Stalin's Soviet Union, Ho Chi Minh's Vietnam, Fidel Castro's Cuba, or Saddam Hussein's Iraq. But the answer is none of these. That distinction belongs to a small, impoverished, and occasionally starving Asian country of 22 million people: North Korea.

Nearly 37,000 Americans, and an estimated three million Koreans, died in the Korean War of 1950–1953, a surrogate world war that was the hot center of the Cold War. It ended without resolution, not in a peace settlement but in a temporary armistice that still holds but has never been more fragile. At the dawn of the twenty-first century, in his January 2002 State of the Union address, President George W. Bush declared North Korea part of an "axis of evil." The following September, a National Security Strategy document issued by his administration referred to two named "rogue states," meaning states beyond the pale, that brutalize their own people, ignore international law, strive to acquire weapons of mass destruction, sponsor terrorism, and "reject basic human values and hate the United States and everything for which it stands." These states, which constituted "a looming threat to all nations," were Iraq and North Korea. Bush has also described North Korea as "the world's most dangerous regime." He told *Washington Post* journalist Bob Woodward that he "loathes" and has a "visceral" reaction to its leader, Kim Jong Il.[1] On other occasions he has referred to him as a "pygmy" and "a spoiled child at a dinner table."[2] With the overthrow of the Saddam Hussein regime in Iraq in April 2003, North Korea is left as a strong contender for the position of Public Enemy Number One.

After five decades of stalemated hostility, peace on the Korean peninsula seems as far away as ever. North Korea maintains a standing army, said to be nearly a million strong, deployed along the Demilitarized Zone (DMZ) barely 30 miles north of the South Korean capital, Seoul. Twelve thousand conventional artillery pieces and some hundreds of Nodong missiles are widely reported to be dug into the hills just above the Demilitarized Zone, capable of devastating Seoul or parts of Japan. The buildup of tension between North Korea and the United States that has gone on over the past year cannot continue. The time is coming when the temporary cease-fire must either be converted into a permanent peace treaty, normalizing the situation on all sides and opening the way to drastic reconstruction of the shattered North Korean economy, or else the militarized, nuclear confrontation may deteriorate into catastrophe.

What kind of state is this bitterest enemy of the United States, and what has its leader done to be so hated? Is it sheer madness that makes him stand defiant before the United States and the world when the devastating consequences are plain? This book explores the origins and character of North Korea, its state and society, its history and present confrontation with the world. It examines the evidence on claims that North Korea has developed nuclear weapons and missiles, but its main interest lies in constructing a frame for understanding the contemporary North Korean phenomenon. If that country seems peculiar-looking indeed to many of the rest of us, that is, in part, because the deepest contradictions and problems of the twentieth century—from imperialism and colonialism to division, war, and nuclear weapons—were left to fester there untended into the twenty-first century. The intensity of North Korea's contemporary defiance reflects the bitterness of its historical experience. Its self-perception is that of a major victim of external aggression. My analysis leads me to conclude that it harbors no aggressive or fanatical threat to the region or the world and that its defiance masks an appeal to normalize relations and "come in from the cold." However, its pride and its sense of the justice of its cause are such that pressure alone is unlikely to lead to resolution. The more the North Koreans are pushed against the wall, the more likely that at some point the regime will feel the desperate urge to strike out. Whether North Korea would be capable of inflicting much damage before being reduced to ashes is another question entirely.

On the surface at least, North Korea is a largely urban, highly educated society, a modern industrial state capable of producing high-tech weapons systems and launching satellites, although uniquely one that has steadily regressed from its modern and industrial status since the 1990s. It looks like no other country on earth. Its behavior patterns are unfamiliar, its rhetoric seems impenetrable, its cult of personality and customs incomprehensible (as was true of China from the 1950s into the 1970s). The images chosen for endless repetition in our media—of goose-stepping soldiers and enormous missiles parading through Pyongyang, of white-coated technicians twiddling knobs at some antiquated-looking nuclear facility, of children, robot-like, performing mass games, of its pudgy leader gesticulating, of starving infants, blank and expressionless—reinforce the sense that it is a place so bizarre as to be beyond the ken of the modern world. What the global media does little to show are the unexotic images of ordinary people going about their difficult daily lives. Sympathy or affection for North Korea is scant to say the least. Apart from South Korea, only neighboring China and Russia, with a stake in the regional order and strong historical ties, show any understanding, however strained.

The Democratic People's Republic of Korea (DPRK), to give North Korea its formal title, is a fossilized "guerrilla state" or "partisan state." Its founding myths and national identity, forged in the 1930s through armed resistance to a brutal Japanese colonialism and further hardened in the bitter contest of the Korean War, have since been maintained by the isolation and unbroken tension of a half century of unresolved confrontation. "Normalcy" has not been known in the area surrounding the Korean peninsula for a hundred years. Because of the wars, hot and cold, that have not ceased since the country's founders took up arms against Japan in the 1930s, North Korea has never demobilized, and it therefore remains an anachronism: permeated in the twenty-first century by guerrilla qualities of secrecy, xenophobia, and leader-centeredness fostered in the 1930s and 1940s. Its "leader" system, political absolutism, and social monolithicity resemble nothing so much as the prewar Japanese emperor system (when one hundred million hearts were said to beat as one). Yet North Korea is no Japan: Fragile, peripheral, and fearful, it attempts to present itself as strong, central, and ferocious in order to attract attention; but aggressive intent is missing.

When the Cold War ended, the peninsula was supposed to stabilize, as communist and former communist countries normalized their relations with South Korea while capitalist and Western countries did likewise with North Korea. But this did not happen. Relations between North Korea and the world's two most important countries, the United States and Japan, remain as abnormal as they were at the moment the Berlin Wall fell. Among contemporary states, North Korea therefore remains Neanderthal, but simply to dismiss it as "evil" is to betray an ignorance of the peculiar historical circumstances that produced it. China and Vietnam have both been divided states (and China, given Taiwan, remains divided), but they have overcome or are in the process of overcoming the passions of horrendous wars and civil wars and are cooperating to build a peaceful future. North and South Korea show every sign of a will to do likewise.

North Korea's military-centered and nuclear preoccupations are dictated above all by the endless siege maintained by the United States. Fearfully and obsessively watching every American move and reacting for half a century to what it perceived as repeated threats of nuclear attack, North Korea absorbed a version of American behavior codes and nuclear values. Its leadership seems to have concluded that the country's (and the regime's) security can only be assured by ironclad, internationally backed guarantees against an American attack; the more the Bush administration dismisses such a demand, the more likely it becomes that North Koreans will be pushed even further along the path of nuclear proliferation. Historically, nuclear threat has always bred nuclear defense, first in Stalin's Soviet Union, convinced there was no other way it could survive, then, England and France responding to the Soviet threat, China to the threat on all sides, India to China, Pakistan to India, and now North Korea to the United States, Jonathan Schell enunciates the general principle, "Deterrence equals proliferation, for deterrence both causes proliferation and is the fruit of it."[3] Each country responds to threat, or perceived threat, by developing its own nuclear capacity, becoming in turn a threat to other nations. Of the nuclear powers only one has actually used nuclear weapons, has consistently brandished them, even against nonnuclear countries, and today pursues research directed at the development of a new generation of "mininukes" and space-based delivery systems designed to cover the entire earth. That one country is, of course, North Korea's nemesis, the United States.

There is little prospect that North Korea can achieve normalcy as a state until its relations with Japan and the United States are normalized, yet both countries insist that North Korea normalize itself first, abandon its nuclear programs, accept inspections, reduce its conventional forces, and so become a "normal" state. If it does these things, it is suggested, then a hand will be extended to welcome the country into the international community, and its grievances and problems will be addressed. However, North Korea has learned that the only way it can attract international attention is precisely by flaunting its weaponry. Moreover, having seen what happened to Iraq—first demonized, then disarmed, pulverized, and occupied when it took steps to comply with similar demands—North Korea insists that only a comprehensive deal can resolve the problems in northeast Asia in general and the Korean peninsula in particular. With the United States and its allies insisting that disarmament is a condition for talks and North Korea insisting it will disarm only as part of a comprehensive settlement, deadlock now prevails.

North Korea points to the hypocrisy of an international system that accepts the development and possession of nuclear weapons by the permanent members of the UN Security Council and implicitly recognizes the same right on the part of a number of additonal states, notably India, Pakistan, and Israel, but denies it to others. For Pyongyang to behave as if it should enjoy the same sort of privilege as a superpower is presumptuous, provocative, and intolerable. However, North Korea has a point. The only principled moral position on this claim is that North Korea should have no such entitlement, but its objections to the hypocrisy of the international nuclear system are well-founded and the task of global nuclear disarmament urgent. No state should have an inherent right to nuclear weapons; but equally no nuclear-armed state has any right to deny others that same prerogative. Only a global movement to achieve universal prohibition can have moral, and in the end political, credibility.

Given the importance of Korea's long struggle for independence from Japan in the colonial period and the centrality of the anti-Japanese guerrilla legends to state and society today, the September 2002 visit to Pyongyang of Japanese Prime Minister Koizumi was a historic event. The Pyongyang declaration that the two leaders issued, while flawed, highlighted a readiness for change on both sides. The promise of the meeting was quickly cut short, however, as a remarkably orchestrated campaign of fear and loathing swept the Japanese media—first over the abductions of Japanese citizens in the 1970s and early 1980s, then over more recent fears that the North Korean regime might threaten Japan with nuclear-armed missiles. Japan, that rare global phenomenon, a constitutional pacifist state, has now taken steps to enable it to launch a war against North Korea, perhaps even preemptively. Yet the North, although armed to the teeth, has not attacked anyone in fifty years, faces explicit threats from the United States, and insists it wants only to survive. Its supposedly mammoth military, touted as the world's fifth-largest force, possesses antiquated equipment, lacks a reliable source of oil supply, and trains soldiers who are desperately hungry. North Korea would have nothing to gain and everything to lose from an attack on Japan, and this book will show that there is nothing in the North Korean record to indicate a suicidal impulse.

The question is this: Is North Korea "a porcupine in the forest repelling aggression" or "a tiger hunting rapaciously in the jungle?"[4] Appearing on Japanese television on June 20, 2003, Hwang Jang-Yop, Kim Jong Il's former mentor and a defector to South Korea, his sworn enemy, insisted that it was absurd to imagine Kim Jong Il ordering an attack on Japan.[5] Better informed than most and yielding to none in his hostility to Kim, Hwang nevertheless favored the porcupine theory.

Most specialists agree that only if its survival seemed immediately threatened would North Korea be likely to lash out. Otherwise, like the porcupine, North Korea simply stiffens its bristles and tries to look as menacing as possible.[6]

North Korea has repeatedly stated that it seeks assurances its sovereignty will be respected and a unilateral attack not be launched against it. This plea is commonly represented as "intimidation" or "blackmail." It may be expressed in the form of a demand, and in strident language, but in itself it is scarcely unreasonable. In fact, no country should feel so vulnerable as to have to seek assurances of a fundamental and universal right. In return for satisfactory assurances to this effect, North Korea has repeatedly offered to give up its nuclear and missile programs. It should not be impossible to satisfy such a desire in a way that enhances, rather than compromises, regional and global peace and security.

In the twenty-first century, Korea may again become the axis for the transformation of state and society in Japan, as it was in the late-nineteenth century when Japan responded to crisis on the Korean peninsula by adopting imperialist and military-first policies. The proponents of forced regime change in North Korea, now dominant in the Japanese government, believe that there can be no resolution of matters at issue so long as the present system remains in Pyongyang. War is a prospect they face with apparent equanimity, and the transformation of Japan into a state capable of fighting such a war is its objective.

Although Washington describes North Korea as a member of the "axis of evil," it would be hard to think of any country as resolutely unilateralist in its ideology and diplomacy, and so unlikely to commit itself to any "axis." "Criminal state," "rogue state," and "outlaw state" are labels that have more credibility, since North Korea seems to have committed almost every crime in the book, from the manufacture and trading of narcotics and missiles, to counterfeiting, smuggling, abductions, spying, and sabotage, while within its own borders it denies its people the most basic rights and freedoms, operates a comprehensive surveillance system, practices severe punishments, including public execution, and confines dissidents to a network of gulag camps. Who outside the country would defend such a record? Remarkably enough, however, North Korea has recently admitted at least some of its crimes (the abductions of Japanese citizens and spy ship intrusions into Japanese waters), apologized for them, and expressed its desire to "go straight" in the future. It has also admitted to developing and possessing nuclear weapons, while insisting it is reluctant about doing so, has no intention of using them, and wants to negotiate their surrender once its security is adequately guaranteed. Other crimes it has not admitted to, but the evidence that it has been involved in smuggling, drug dealing, and currency counterfeiting is so strong as to be virtually undeniable, and there is a strong circumstantial reason to suspect that it may also have been involved in major terrorist attacks in the 1980s.

Yet simply to label North Korea "terrorist" is neither to grasp the burden of the past, nor to offer any prescription for the present or future. Criminality is not so unusual in relations between states, but apology is. It seems hard to imagine why Kim Jong Il would have taken the bold steps he did in 2002 unless he wanted to clear the slate and move toward comprehensive normalization. Instead, his apologies attracted a torrent of abuse and a hardening of hostility against him, forcing him, in turn, to revert to a hard-line position.

The Western image of North Korea as brutal and beyond the pale is rooted in the Korean War of 1950–1953. It was a determining moment. The whole of Korea, North and South, was physically devastated. On both sides the national aspiration to create a unified state was blunted for a generation as the divided North and South became locked into subordinate roles in the Cold War, internalizing its passions and its logic.

While the popular Western images of and understanding of the war have scarcely changed in half a century, specialist studies have now made it clear how deeply flawed that understanding is. The war was indeed started by North Korea and supported by Soviet dictator Joseph Stalin. However, it was not a Russian push for regional hegemony in east Asia so much as a civil war between two rival Korean regimes that stemmed from the external division of the peninsula imposed in 1945 on a people just emerging from decades of brutal colonial rule. Not only was the United Nations deeply involved in the events leading to war, but for the only time in its history it actually became a protagonist in the fighting. It therefore bears a peculiar and continuing responsibility for the Korean dilemma. The representation of the war as one of civilization against barbarism, international justice against an outlaw state, was fundamentally false. We now know that many of the greatest atrocities in that awful war were committed by the South Koreans and the United States—at Nogunri, Taejon, and elsewhere—and then by the United States alone, when in its air campaign against the North it devastated dams, power stations, and the infrastructure of social life in breach of international law. In other words, if it was a terror war, much of the terror was inflicted by the forces acting in the name of the United Nations.

While the United States and Japanese approaches to North Korea favor a tightening of the screws to induce submission, backed by the ultimate threat of force, South Korea prefers a "Sunshine" approach, favoring dialogue and stressing long-term national unity, while fostering economic, cultural, and other contacts. Its greatest success so far has been the restoration of a north-south rail link, ruptured since 1950. Although by the end of 2003 the service was ready to resume and both North and South wanted it, it was far from clear when the trains would actually run.

"Sunshine" is clearly welcome to North Korea, which has given many indications that it is seeking a way in from the cold. In the wake of the September 11, 2001, terror attacks, it ratified the international anti-terror conventions and it has begun to report internationally on its obligations under the International Covenant on Civil and Political Rights.[7] It has also been struggling for more than a decade to reengage its economy with the world. Economic reform and political liberalization are, however, impossible as long as North Korea faces security threats that continue to require a huge military system, and so long as it is denied access to international institutions such as the World Bank and the International Monetary Fund, to which the United States holds the keys. Only when peace is reached with Japan and the United States can there be any prospect of this structure being dissolved.

Pyongyang's rhetoric, shrill to the point of incomprehensibility, has commonly been interpreted as a language of "blackmail" or "intimidation," to which the United States will not yield. But North Korea's behavior might better be interpreted as a structurally conditioned overreaction. Facing the concentrated hostility of the globe's only superpower and bereft of any significant diplomatic support, weakness and fear are masked by bluster, provocative language, and aggressive gesture. An aggrieved sense of injustice on the part of North Korea as the weaker party serves only to heighten the rhetorical tone. This is a country one-third the size of the state of California, with an economy equal to that of Alameda County in the San Francisco Bay area.[8] Such outward signs should not be confused with the growl of the tiger. Restraint, and a serious effort to find ways in which North Korea could preserve some "face" while proceeding with needed drastic reforms, would be the wise way for the globe's only superpower to respond.

The contemporary crisis is so deep that only a radical leap of the imagination could suffice to conceive of any resolution, yet the very intractability of the situation may also be a source of hope. As east Asia faces the peremptory challenge of adapting to the new American imperium, the voices of an alternative regional order begin to be heard, emanating from surprisingly diverse quarters. The one thing on which Tokyo, Seoul, and Pyongyang express clear agreement is the need to move toward some kind of regional east Asian (or Asian) community. Having been at the center of the three great attempts at regional and global systems in the twentieth century—Japanese fascism in its first half and capitalist and communist Cold War empires in its second—Korea may now find itself at the center of an emerging post–twentieth century order.

Like spring to a frozen river, change is undoubtedly coming to North Korea. Its course is unpredictable, in part because of the length and depth of the freeze. The election of Kim Dae Jung as president of South Korea in 1997 and his pro-engagement Sunshine policy, which broke with decades of hostility toward the North, provided the beleaguered DPRK with an opportunity to seek openings for desperately needed capital investment. Pyongyang entered negotiations, proud yet nervously vulnerable, always mindful of its exceedingly local military advantage as a bargaining chip. In June 2000, Kim Dae Jung traveled north for a historic summit with Kim Jong Il. Both pledged social, economic, and cultural cooperation and joint progress toward reunification, in an atmosphere of peninsula-wide euphoric anticipation. Since then, despite every crisis, the web of negotiation and cooperation between South and North has steadily thickened.

To strive to understand North Korea in terms of the peculiar circumstances out of which it has evolved does not mean to justify its system. It scarcely needs to be said that the major victims of the system are not outsiders but the people of North Korea. There is general agreement on many of the basic facts. Between one and two million—5 to 10 percent—are estimated to have died of starvation, and hundreds of thousands of refugees have fled, mostly to China. Early in 2003 UNICEF reported that in a population of about 22 million, 15 million women and children "continue to need external assistance to survive and grow," one-third of mothers are malnourished and anemic, 9 percent of children suffer wasting or acute malnutrition, and 42 percent stunting or chronic malnutrition.[9] Up to 200,000 people—just under 1 percent of the population—are thought to be held in labor camps.

Although North Korea's peculiar blend of terror, mobilization, and seclusion has been slowly losing its coherence since the end of the Cold War, the system is still held together by the absolute authority of the "Dear Leader" and by an ideology (however founded in historical reality) of Japanese and American perfidy. The continued hostility of both countries helps to maintain the garrison state, while high levels of tension and fear help legitimize and sustain the closed, totalitarian system. Such a system does not deserve to continue, but as the record in Afghanistan and Iraq shows, the attempt to resolve complex problems of violence and terror by counterviolence and counterterror offers no prospect of a lasting solution.

The invasion of Iraq in 2003 showed that preventive force may easily unseat a dictator, but success in that straightforward mission has to be measured against its other consequences—deepening crisis in the Middle East, spreading terror, and the possible proliferation of nuclear and other weapons of mass destruction. Furthermore, if a "preventive" attack, however "limited," were launched on North Korea's nuclear facilities and missile sites, as Washington's neocons have long urged, the military response would undoubtedly be formidable, since North Korea preserves the sort of military capability long ago given up by Iraq. The other favored neocon path—ratcheting up the pressure to force the collapse of the North Korean regime—is also an extremely dubious proposition. Both South Korea and China fear that an economic implosion in Pyongyang could spread chaos through the region and perhaps bring on a global, economic catastrophe.

The priority the Bush administration gives to solving problems by violence or pressure tends to shift attention from the other paths that are open—paths neither utopian nor dreamy, but realistic and capable in the long run of profoundly changing North Korea, the east Asian region, and even perhaps the United States for the better. It is not too late to avoid the catastrophe of North Korea brought low in the worst possible way or to avoid capping that with a final catastrophe beyond measure. There are ways out of this global bind, all of which involve understanding where the parties involved have come from, the history that lies behind their present stances, and the aspirations they share.

# THE WAR THAT WAS, 1950–1953

The Korean War was a civil war that foreign intervention turned into a surrogate world war. Americans and Russians (in Chinese uniforms) battled in the skies, while on the ground British, Australians, Turks, and others fought as part of a U.S.–led "coalition of the willing" against North Korean regulars and Chinese "volunteers." The fighting began on the morning of June 25, 1950, when Korean People's Army (KPA) forces crossed into the South. American power in the world was then such that it was able to secure resolutions committing the United Nations itself to war, sending a sixteen-nation force under the UN flag and U.S. command to block the North Korean aggression. Although Seoul was captured within a few days, the tide slowly turned against the North Korean army, and three months later the UN forces had driven them back across the 38th parallel and toward the Chinese frontier, prompting the intervention of the "Chinese People's Volunteers." The two sides fought on, contesting barren hillsides and wrangling interminably over issues of face and ideology, until an eventual truce was signed on July 27, 1953, the demarcation line dividing South from North was drawn almost exactly where it had been when the war began.

It was a war without a victor, which only exacerbated the problems that gave rise to it. It ended in a stalemate of exhaustion, the country laid waste to such an extent that it would take a generation to recover economically; the psychological and emotional healing goes on still. It was the opening round in a struggle for regional and global advantage between the United States and China. And for the United States, like September 11 half a century later, war in Korea was the trigger for a huge shift from the containment of a hostile ideology and system to its "rollback," from a peace to a war economy. There is no way to make sense of the present face-off in the Koreas without backing up to look at what led to the Korean War.

The simple answer to the question of why there was a war in 1950 is that the United States, to suit its global needs, divided a country that had been united for over a thousand years and whose culture and tradition were extraordinarily coherent. Soviet forces crossed the border into Korea on August 9, 1945, and by the time the Japanese surrendered six days later, had already captured much of northern Korea, while the nearest United States forces were hundreds of kilometers away on the island of Okinawa. Hastily, in the State Department an arbitrary line was drawn across the map at the 38$^{th}$ parallel, a geographical marker of no previous political or cultural significance, which had the effect of placing Korea's capital, Seoul, and most of its population under American influence. Despite the fact that the Americans had no troops on the ground, Russian dictator Joseph Stalin acquiesced in ordering his forces to withdraw to the U.S. line. Had European precedent been followed, as with Germany, so Japan, the aggressor state in Asia would have been divided and occupied; instead, it was Korea, the victim of nearly half a century of brutal Japanese colonial rule, that was divided. For Koreans this act of division was the original sin—and the cause of their long travails through the rest of the century.

The twentieth century was filled with pain for Koreans. The first half of the century was spent under a concentrated Japanese effort to incorporate them into Japan itself and the second half coping with the consequences of the division that followed Japan's defeat in 1945. Not only did Japan impose a government on them between 1910 and 1945, it also strove to extinguish their national identity, substitute the worship of the Japanese emperor and his ancestors as the state religion, replace Korean names and the Korean language with Japanese names and the Japanese language, and, as Japan moved to total mobilization during World War 2, to mobilize young Korean men into Japan's armed forces or to work in mines and at construction sites, and tens of thousands of young women, most of them between the ages of sixteen and nineteen as "comfort women" to service sexually the Imperial Japanese Army.

The "vacuum" in Korea, caused in August 1945 when the Japanese imperial order collapsed, was filled by Koreans burning with desire for national liberation and social change. In the North, under Stalin's sponsorship, a regime with strong anti-Japanese credentials was formed, but in the South nationalist groups were mercilessly suppressed. Koreans below the 38th parallel who welcomed liberation from Japanese imperialism as the fulfillment of their national destiny and embraced it as an opportunity to implement an independent, just Korean social order were forced instead to accept a subordinate state whose *raison d'être* was anticommunism, not independence. The objectives of American policy-makers were negative and preemptive: to deny as much of Korean territory as possible to the Soviet Union and to establish a cooperative regime that would reflect U.S. strategic interests. Fearful above all of a unified communist Korea, nationalist aspiration was anathema to the Americans and had to be crushed, just as similar aspirations would later be crushed by the Soviet Union in Hungary and Czechoslovakia.

With the announcement of the Japanese surrender, the capital, Seoul, was swept by joyful anticipation and a spontaneous network of popular local organizations, the "People's Committees," emerged as the core of a prospective new national order intent on rooting out the supporters and beneficiaries of the old order and creating a more just and equitable society. These two aspirations might potentially have led to a radical transformation of society of a kind that classically had given birth to new democratic nation-states, but it was not to be. The People's Committees were quickly banned as a "communist front," and the archconservative and staunch anticommunist Syngman Rhee, an *émigré* Korean who had lived for decades in Washington, developing strong ties to conservative Americans, was imposed at the head of a new regime.

The state structures that Rhee and his American mentors built fused their ideological anticommunism with the conservatism of rural Korean elites and underpinned it all with a revamped security and police apparatus inherited from the old Japanese colonial state. With his autocratic and conservative elite background, close American connections, and commitment to the new "rollback" phase of anticommunism, Rhee became the perfect symbol of the new order.

Within months of their arrival, therefore, the Americans were widely reviled. General Hodge, the U.S. military commander, recognized that "pro-American" had become an epithet akin to "pro-Jap national traitor, and Jap collaborator." Hodge's intelligence told him in February 1946 that leftist elements in the South would be bound to win any fair election, and in that same month a survey found that 49 percent of South Koreans felt that conditions were worse under the Americans than they had been under the Japanese.[1]

Those associated with the People's Committees and an incipient republic were frozen out of power, then arrested or driven underground. In the autumn of 1946 South Korea

*Chicago Sun* correspondent Mark Gayn described a situation that threatened to turn into "a full-scale revolution," involving "hundreds of thousands, if not millions of people."[2] Uncoordinated peasant or urban attempts to defend the People's Committees, or even to seize local and provincial power, were, however, no match for the Japanese-trained security forces; many were killed. The most prominent figure committed to forging a broad national consensus and seeking accommodation with the north, Yo Unhyong, was assassinated in July 1947.

On November 11, 1947, Patrick Shaw, then head of the Australian diplomatic mission in Tokyo, described the situation in South Korea:

> Real power is apparently in the hands of the ruthless police force which works at the direction of the G2 Section of the American G.HQ and Syngman Rhee and Kim Koo [Kim Koo was a prominent Korean nationalist who returned to Korea in 1945 from China, where he had been part of the anti-Japanese "Korean Provisional Government"]. Korean prisons are now fuller of political prisoners than under Japanese rule. The torture and murder of the political enemies of the extreme Right is apparently an accepted and commonplace thing.

In the Soviet zone, a higher degree of autonomy was initially allowed, and aspirations for national and social liberation were encouraged. Radical but broadly popular social and economic reforms were implemented, including the purge of Japanese collaborators, land reform, the emancipation of women, and the transfer to public ownership of all Japanese assets. In the contest between Soviet and Korean influences, a recent study by Columbia University scholar Charles Armstrong concludes that there was more Koreanization of Soviet communism than

Sovietization of North Korea: "North Korea became Stalinist in form, but was clearly nationalist in content."[3] This is not to imply that Soviet policy was dictated by any particular virtue, merely to recognize that Soviet interests were then served by giving freer rein to the revolutionary dynamism of Korean society. Stalin did not need to intervene.

Kim Il Sung, who emerged at the head of this new structure, would remain the dominant figure in North Korea for the next four and a half decades. As a guerrilla leader of the anti-Japanese struggle of the 1930s, his anti-Japanese credentials were impeccable. If he was hardly the godlike figure of "infinite genius" Pyongyang likes to represent him as, he had at least fought against Japan, had ability and drive, was highly regarded by both Chinese and Soviet authorities, having served as an officer in both the Chinese and the Soviet communist armies, and not least he was favored by circumstances and luck.

## THE UNITED NATIONS

Late in 1947, thanks to a unilateral American initiative, the problem of the now-divided Korea was transferred to the United Nations, in which American dominance was then at a peak. A UN Temporary Commission for Korea (UNTCOK) was set up, supposedly to see to the holding of elections for a National Assembly not later than March 31, 1948. Thus commenced the involvement of the UN in a rolling, roiling Korean crisis that was to lead, in due course, to a step it has never otherwise taken; the direct prosecution of a war.

It was almost immediately clear that cooperation from the Soviet Union would be unlikely, and indeed UN requests to enter the Northern sector were rebuffed. As the Commission, nonetheless, saw its role as supervision of *national* elections, it proved initially, according to its chair, India's K.P. Menon, "all but unanimous" in opposition to separate, *sectoral* elections. On February 26, however, the UN's Interim Committee (the standing committee of the General Assembly set up to advise on matters of peace and security in 1947) met in New York, just as a communist coup was taking place in Czechoslovakia. Some members at least were persuaded that the communists must be prevented from "winning" in Korea as they had in Czechoslovakia, and so endorsed the idea of "national elections even without Soviet support."[4]

When the members of UNTCOK had arrived in Korea early in 1948, they proved extremely reluctant to endorse separate Southern elections, but sustained U.S. pressure was applied. The decision to conduct elections was adopted two months later for such parts of the country as were accessible, provided there existed "a reasonable degree of free atmosphere," it was carried by the barest of margins, against Canadian and Australian opposition and with the crucial Indian vote cast in favor because, as the Indian delegate later wrote, he had been "open to persuasion." He had in fact been persuaded against his better judgment by his Korean lover, a well-known woman poet.[5] The delegates who insisted that such elections would not advance the cause of Korean unification and would be boycotted by "all but the extreme right" were denounced by General Hodge for "general appeasement of Soviet Russia." History nevertheless proved them right on both counts.

As separate elections loomed, the most prominent members of the Southern leadership, except for Syngman Rhee, wrote to Kim Il Sung to propose a North-South political conference. The Australian and Canadian delegates declared their support for the idea and such a conference was indeed held in Pyongyang in April, with 240 Southern delegates, including the most prominent liberal and rightist nationalist leaders. However, its joint declaration, calling for the immediate withdrawal of all foreign troops, rejection of "dictatorship and monopoly capitalism," and the formation of a united government, was overtaken by events.

Boycotted by the left and the nationalist right, the Southern elections, organized by the National Police and associated rightist groups, were held on May 10, after a campaign of officially sponsored violence and intimidation. None of the UNTCOK members considered the parliament that resulted to be a national institution. Even after seven weeks of debate and continuing U.S. pressure, agreement could only be reached on an ambiguous formula that declared the elections "a valid expression of the free will of the electorate in those parts of Korea which were accessible to the Commission." The elected representatives were nevertheless convened as a national assembly, a constitution was drawn up, and Syngman Rhee was installed as president of the "Republic of Korea." On August 12, the U.S. government recognized this as the government envisaged in the 1947 United Nations resolution and on December 12 the UN General Assembly followed suit, declaring the new body "the only legal government in Korea."

The Republic of Korea (ROK) was thus born in inauspicious circumstances, marked by violence, repression, and the exercise of consistent and determined U.S. pressure on the UN and its Commission.[6] Widespread discontent over this entrenching of division exploded on the island of Cheju, off Korea's southern coast. As a result, between 10 and 25 percent of its 300,000 inhabitants were massacred, more than half of their villages burned, and the panoply of anti-guerrilla measures later developed to the full in Vietnam—herding of the population into strategic hamlets or fortified villages, destruction of crops, scorched earth, slaughter of villagers—put into operation.[7] Only after the uprising had been mercilessly suppressed could "elections" be held on Cheju, one year later than the rest of the country.

Pyongyang held its own elections on August 25 and established, as a rival institution, a Supreme People's Assembly, which also claimed legitimacy as a national parliament, and a government headed by Kim Il Sung. The United Nations's intervention had only reinforced the division of the peninsula. Of the two hostile regimes, one preserved largely intact the central features of the Japanese colonial state and the organs on which that state had rested, while the other was created out of forces that had struggled for decades against Japan and gave form to deeply felt demands for radical social and economic reform. The fact that the Soviet Union and China backed it overshadowed at the time the primacy of Korean nationalism in the North. The diametrically opposed paths followed by the two zones of occupation gradually weakened any prospects for unification, since the merging of a revolutionary and a counter-revolutionary regime could have only been achieved by the surrender of one side or by war.

A temporary and *de facto* division had been converted into one that was enduring and *de jure*. By 1950, two irreconcilable regimes, gathering their strength, faced each other across the 38th Parallel, both committed to unification by force. When Korea exploded in 1950 it was Kim Il Sung who initiated the invasion in the attempt to unify the sundered nation, but Syngman Rhee had often threatened it and had even launched cross-border raids in 1949 to test Northern defenses. Despite what was believed at the time, Stalin had no plan for world conquest and gave his consent to the invasion plans only reluctantly, after forty-eight telegraphic pleas from Kim.[8]

### The War Begins

Korea had two governments, communist and anticommunist, each determined to extend its writ over the whole country. In the South in 1948, a reorganized United Nations Commission (UNCOK) was supposed to lend its good offices to promote reunification, to be available for "observation and consultation" as free and representative institutions developed, and in due course to observe the withdrawal of foreign troops. In fact, its capacity to exert leverage over the Republic of Korea government in the South was slight, and with the Democratic People's Republic of Korea government, nonexistent.

UNCOK delegates in Seoul were frustrated by their inability to influence events and disturbed by the repressive nature of the regime. The Indian and Australian delegates in particular were concerned over arrests of national assemblymen, intimidation of the press, and "the fact that public meetings frequently could not take place." Guerrilla warfare continued in the countryside, and in areas in which guerrilla activity had been crushed, order was maintained "only through police state machinery of espionage, censorship, propaganda, and repression."[9] In June 1948, the rightist leader, Kim Ku [Koo], who had visited Pyongyang in April and been denounced by Syngman Rhee as a "traitor," was assassinated. The murders of Yo Unhyong and Kim removed two outstanding South Korean noncommunist nationalist leaders, one of the left and one of the right, each passionately opposed to any splitting of the nation.

According to the head of the Australian Mission in Tokyo, the government was "an arbitrary dictatorship of the president and a few members of the Cabinet, enforced by ruthless police action." The CIA thought Rhee "senile," if also "indomitably strong-willed and obstinate," while in the British embassy he was regarded as "a dangerous fascist, or lunatic."[10] Large-scale campaigns for the suppression of resistance within South Korea continued through early 1950. Walter Sullivan wrote in the *New York Times* that spring of the country being "darkened by a cloud of terror that is probably unparalleled in the world." Rhee grew even more strident in his calls for a "march" north to unify the country and his forces stepped up raids. He boasted that it would take him just three days to capture the northern capital, Pyongyang. Australia's Department of External Affairs in Canberra noted: "The [Seoul] Government's only proposed solution to the problem of unification is bullets and bayonets,"[11] a comment at least as true of the North as of the South.

In April, Kim visited Moscow, where Stalin gave his final seal of approval to the "Preemptive Strike Operational Pan."[12] At the beginning of May, Kim Il Sung visited the new leader of the People's Republic of China, Mao Zedong, the victor in the Chinese civil war, to gain his support for the plans. Mao seems to have thought U.S. intervention unlikely. Between the summer of 1949 and the next spring, the Chinese People's Liberation Army released some 50,000 to 70,000 ethnic Korean soldiers, all battle-hardened veterans, to return to the North with their military equipment.[13] Secret telegraphic exchanges between Pyongyang and Moscow confirmed an agreement to supply equipment not just for the Korean People's Army's seven existing infantry divisions, but for three new ones, "so long as success is completely guaranteed." The promised Soviet weapons and equipment, including tanks, arrived in April by sea and road from Vladivostok.[14] Early in the morning of June 25, Northern forces rolled across the 38th Parallel. The war had begun.

Hastily convened in New York on June 25, the Security Council passed an American resolution denouncing the North Korean "armed attack," calling on North Korea to withdraw and on member states to cooperate to achieve that goal. With no independent sources of information, the Council simply accepted what it was told by the American ambassador. From the account given by Secretary-General Trygve Lie, we know that he personally intervened to persuade several Council members to vote for the U.S. resolution,[15] and from a "Top Secret, Emergency" cable dispatched to its government by the Australian mission in New York it appears that the French and Egyptian delegates were also persuaded to change their votes, based on information that "ten of the twenty captured tanks were not only of Russian origin but were actually manned by Russian troops."[16] That report was obviously a fabrication, since no Russian prisoners were produced at any stage of the war. The vote was carried nine to zero, with one abstention and in the fortuitous absence of the Soviet Union, then boycotting the Council in protest against its refusal to transfer the China seat to Beijing. It could otherwise have vetoed any action.

Since the Korean dispute was one between two rival claimants to national sovereignty—that is, a civil war—strictly speaking the peace enforcement powers of the Security Council should not have applied. But a second resolution, actually committing the UN to war, was passed two days later. Trygve Lie indicated on this occasion that he did indeed have independent evidence to prove the American allegations—in the form of a report written on the eve of war by two Australian officers from a UN Field Observer mission sent to the 38th parallel early in June.[17] Their report, however, merely stated that they had seen no sign of war preparations on either side of the parallel.

It was enough to persuade UNCOK, meeting in Seoul on June 26, to advise the secretary-general that the Northern regime was carrying out a "well-planned, concerted, and full-scale invasion of south Korea." The logic was this: Since there was no evidence that the Southern side had been preparing an invasion, therefore the Northern side must have been responsible. It was this UNCOK interpretation, not the Field Observers's text, that reached the UN Security Council and was crucial in its second debate. Both men, interviewed by this author in 1982, agreed that, in effect, they had seen nothing.

The "coalition of the willing," formed in response to the UN resolution, comprised sixteen nations under U.S. command. In the early weeks of the war, the North Korean People's Army advanced with lightning speed, taking the Southern capital, Seoul, on day four of the invasion, although American military headquarters estimated that the attacking army of about

38,000 was outnumbered by the 50,000 Southern troops in the region between Seoul and the 38th parallel.[18] The South Korean government quickly fled south (the special assistant to the UN Secretary-General, Colonel Alfred Katzin, described Rhee and his government as "a useless mob"), relocating to Pusan, while allied forces retreated steadily, to a defense perimeter along the Naktong River. The North Korean gamble was that the outbreak of war would precipitate a total political collapse in the South and victory so speedy that an international intervention could not be organized in time. It quickly captured some 95 percent of the national territory and 98 percent of the population, but those final few percentage points were its undoing. It was not ready to face the full power of the American military or for the kind of prolonged warfare that then ensued.

U.S. strategic thinking in early 1950 was undergoing an important shift, which would make Kim Il Sung's venture immeasurably more hazardous than he anticipated. The "double shocks" of communist victory in the Chinese civil war and the successful explosion of the first Soviet nuclear weapon shook Washington. National Security Council 68 (NSC 68), a top-level, secret memorandum submitted to President Truman on April 12, 1950, outlined a Manichean view of a struggle against a "fanatic" Kremlin design for world hegemony, a spiritual antecedent of the worldview of the neo-conservatives of the present administration. NSC 68 called for increasing taxes and doubling or tripling the defense budget, while laying the groundwork for a strategic shift from the containment of the "rollback" of communism.[19]

## FIGHTING THE WAR

The "Inchon Landing" of General Douglas MacArthur, the Washington-appointed commander of the UN forces in Korea, reversed the tides of war, effectively severing the supply lines of the Northern army. Air attacks and a gradual buildup of men and material on the UN side only intensified the pressure. The North Korean forces collapsed almost as suddenly as they had exploded across the border less than three months earlier. By the end of September, Rhee was back in Seoul, his hopes of dominating a united Korea now soaring. By mid-October, Stalin was advising Kim Il Sung to prepare to evacuate his forces to either the Soviet Union or China.[20]

The UN forces might, of course, have rested content with dispatching Kim Il Sung's army back across the 38th parallel, but American policy-makers, in their rollback mode, were resolved on pursuing it across the old frontier and destroying the northern regime. A resolution calling for "all appropriate steps" to be taken to establish a unified, independent, democratic Korea was adopted in the General Assembly, and a UN Commission for the Unification and Rehabilitation of Korea was set up. However, the rush of the U.S.–led UN forces toward the Chinese and Soviet borders not only threatened the extinction of the Kim Il Sung regime but also carried the distinct risk of widening the conflict.

As the first American troops neared the Yalu River at the Chinese frontier, concern mounted in Beijing. Mao Zedong had not anticipated the catastrophic reverses that now threatened the survival of Kim's government. Reluctance to commit Chinese forces outside the country when national reconstruction after a long civil war was at stake had to be balanced against the risks of a hostile U.S.–dominated government on China's doorstep—and even the invasion of China itself.

After sixty sleepless hours brooding on the likely costs, including the possible nuclear devastation of China's cities, on October 13 Mao made up his mind. A surrogate war would be better than a direct war. A Chinese force of 250,000 men crossed the Yalu River frontier and launched a massive counteroffensive, forcing a retreat that for a time seemed likely to turn into a rout. On December 5, Pyongyang recaptured, once again the decision was taken to ignore the division line at the 38th parallel and strive for total victory rather than negotiate a settlement. On Christmas Day, the combined force of the KPA and the Chinese People's Volunteers crossed the 38th parallel and soon afterward recaptured Seoul.

Late in 1950, the Soviet Union also directly if surreptitiously entered the war. Not until 1989 was it officially admitted that a Soviet Air Force unit had fought in Korea. The Russian pilots and their 200 MIG fighters left Moscow in mid-November. They operated in the northern parts of North Korea, dressed in Chinese uniforms, with Chinese markings on their planes and only flew missions over territory controlled by North Korean or Chinese forces. Although their losses, especially initially, were heavy, they claim to have shot down over 1,300 U.S. planes, damaging hundreds more for losses of 345 of their own.[21] The unit commander himself, Lt. General Georgy Lobov, is said to have shot down fourteen U.S. planes.[22] Whatever the accuracy of this, for two and a half years a secret but full-scale war would be fought between the United States and the Soviet Union in Korean, Chinese, and Soviet skies, involving thousands of aircraft.

What had begun as a civil conflict between North and South had now massively expanded due to the intervention, first of the United States, then of the other nations that made up the United Nations Command, next of China, and finally of the Soviet Union. A Japanese coastguard unit also became involved in a top secret mission to clear North Korean harbors of mines to facilitate the northward push.[23] The Korean civil war had now become the Cold War in miniature, fought with almost total abandon.

## WEAPONS OF MASS DESTRUCTION
The American mood turned from optimism to gloom and

desperation when the Chinese assault sent U.S. forces into full-scale retreat. On the pattern of the Chinese Nationalist evacuation of Mainland China for Taiwan at the end of the Chinese civil war, American planners even considered the bizarre idea of establishing a "new Korea" by relocating 328,000 South Koreans to the remote islands of Savaii and Upolu in the South Pacific.[24] Far more seriously, since defeat seemed an inconceivable option now that the Korean War had been reconceived as a global struggle with Communism, they also considered escalation.

As the tide of battle turned against United Nations forces, the use of nuclear weapons was put on the table. On November 30, President Truman publicly announced that their use was under active consideration, adding that he saw no need for UN authorization. This caused such consternation among America's allies that British Prime Minister Clement Attlee flew to Washington to urge restraint. In fact, Truman was considering not only the use of the bomb, but also an air assault on China and a blockade of its coast, while the Joint Chiefs of Staff were contemplating assisting the defeated Chinese Nationalists on Taiwan in an effort to recapture the mainland. On December 9, MacArthur, asked for twenty-six atomic bombs and the right to use them at his discretion, listing Beijing, Dairen, and Port Arthur in China and the Russian cities of Vladivostok and Khabarovsk as possible targets. He also developed a plan to "end" the war in ten days by dropping atomic bombs across the "neck" of Manchuria north of Korea's Yalu River frontier, introducing half a million Kuomintang troops from Taiwan, and then spreading a belt of radioactive cobalt from the Sea of Japan to the Yellow Sea.[25] Had MacArthur implemented his plan, world war would almost certainly have resulted, and much of Korea (at least) would have been rendered uninhabitable.

Despite his assurances to Prime Minister Attlee, Truman did

order atomic bombs to be sent, unassembled, to aircraft carriers off the Korean coast and bases on Okinawa. In January he confided to his diary that he contemplated destroying "Moscow and every manufacturing plant in China and the Soviet Union."[26] However, doubt about whether the bomb could be effective in Korea, given the gradual deepening of Chinese and Korean defensive bunkers and tunnels—ultimately a 1,250-kilometer labyrinth—and a reluctance about risking world war, were major considerations. There was also uncertainty over whether nuclear weapons could be used "safely," given the closeness of the opposing forces. In addition, American planners feared the possibility of the Soviet Union being drawn into nuclear retaliation, perhaps against Japan. Moral scruples, or concern over possible infringement of international law, seem to have played no role in the deliberations.

Nuclear weapons were seriously considered from time to time thereafter. In May 1951, one month after President Truman dismissed General MacArthur for insubordination, his successor, General Matthew Ridgway, sought authorization for their use.[27] Later in 1951, under "Operation Hudson Harbor," simulated nuclear bombing runs over Pyongyang were launched by B-29s, meant to mimic the atomic bombings of Hiroshima and Nagasaki at the end of World War II and so to be stark and terrifying warnings. The question was debated periodically thereafter at the highest levels of government. Between March and May 1953 the option was seriously debated. The Joint Chiefs of Staff recommended their use to the new president, Dwight D. Eisenhower, who had won the election in part on a pledge "to go to Korea" that was widely interpreted to mean he would end the war. In May, however, Eisenhower agreed, attracted by the fact that the nuclear option was "cheaper dollar-wise" than conventional methods.[28] He believed that "it would be impossible . . . to maintain military commitments around the world . . . did we not possess atomic weapons *and the will to use them*" (italics added).[29] Ultimately allied pressure, a pragmatic concern over the possibility of Soviet retaliation, and a breakthrough in the peace talks saved Korea (and possibly the world) from nuclear conflagration. The threat of unleashing the awesome power of nuclear weapons was, however, burned into North Korean imagination during these years.

Korea thus escaped nuclear attack. The question of whether bacteriological ("germ") warfare was employed by the Americans proved far more controversial at the time—and since. The allegation was first made by the Chinese-North Korean side in May 1951, after smallpox and typhoid had broken out in areas abandoned by U.S. troops retreating from North Korea. In February 1952, the further claim was made that low-flying U.S. planes had dropped bacterial bombs designed to disseminate plague, typhoid, anthrax, and other diseases. "Confessions" of captured U.S. airmen were broadcast in support of the allegations, and details of locations, casualties, and types of bacteria and mechanisms of conveyance were published.[30]

The charge that the United States had resorted to bacteriological warfare seemed plausible for a number of circumstantial reasons. Huge stockpiles of sarin nerve gas were actually readied for possible use[31] and, although the United States firmly denied it, it did have a significant biological warfare capacity. It had even secretly experimented during the 1950s with the dissemination of supposedly biological agents in places like the New York City subway system and the Pentagon water supply. After the Japanese surrender in 1945, it had also gone to considerable lengths to secure the fruits of the large-scale Japanese biological and chemical warfare program in China. Unit 731 of the Imperial Japanese Army was the embodiment of the most depraved and criminal qualities of that wartime fascist state and, by giving immunity and protection to its principals in return for their secrets, documents, and samples, Washington became complicit after the fact in its crimes.

When the Soviet Union in 1949 held trials of some captured members of this unit, the United States denounced the trials as a fraudulent and absurd fabrication, so that the truth did not emerge until the 1970s, when former members of the unit began to confess and documents released under the Freedom of Information Act confirmed virtually every detail originally published in the Soviet trials. With the U.S. lie about its knowledge of biological warfare thus dramatically exposed, its denials of biological warfare in Korea had to be reconsidered, especially because the pathogens and delivery systems allegedly employed in Korea seemed to be closely modeled on the Japanese precedents.

There also was a scientific report in 1952 that found the United States guilty of such crimes. The "International Scientific Commission for the Investigation of the Facts Concerning Bacterial Warfare in Korea and China," organized under the auspices of the World Peace Council, had experts from Brazil, Britain, France, Italy, Sweden, and the Soviet Union. It conducted investigations in Korea and China between June and August 1952 and published a 700-page report in English in Peking in 1952. It was attacked at the time as "fellow-traveling," but its scientists's credentials were impressive, perhaps the most outstanding being the Cambridge embryologist (and later eminent historian of Chinese science) Joseph Needham. As a scientific liaison officer in the British embassy in China during the Sino-Japanese war, Needham had studied the Japanese biological attacks in central China and believed he was seeing the same techniques employed in Korea. However, the Commission was heavily dependent on the cooperation of Chinese scientists and became embroiled in very controversial matters by hearing, and apparently accepting, the evidence of captured U.S.

pilots (all of whom later recanted when the pilots were freed).

The matter therefore remained for long open to doubt, especially since the episodes alleged did not seem to make military sense. If the United States had really engaged in biological warfare, it did so in an amateurish, ineffective way, employing a puzzling array of pathogens and producing few victims, and despite the passage of time, no corroborative evidence turned up either in the archives or in the form of testimony from participants in such a program.

In the early 1990s, however, a batch of twelve documents from the archives of the former Soviet Union provided a fragmentary, but persuasive, explanation of what had actually happened.[32] Analysis of these documents makes it seem almost certain that there was a vigorous, complex, contrived, and fraudulent international campaign on the part of the North Koreans, the Chinese, and the Russians—a gigantic fraud or "a patriotic conspiracy" of a sort that Joseph Needham had believed inconceivable.[33] "False areas of infection" were deliberately created. People sentenced to death were deliberately infected with cholera bacteria taken from corpses in plague-infested areas of China, presumably then killed and their bodies dumped at strategic locations. To quote only one of the documents, a communication from the Soviet government to Mao Zedong in May 1953 began as follows:

> For Mao: The Soviet Government and the Central Committee of the CPSU were misled. The spread in the press of information about the use of bacteriological weapons in Korea was based on false information. The accusations against the Americans were fictitious.

When Mao was apprised of this by a special delegation from Moscow, he "smoked a lot, crushed cigarettes, and drank a lot of tea." Who originated the conspiracy remains unknown, but the motive may be surmised: the desire to weaken the coalition fighting the war against them by fomenting an international movement of moral outrage, perhaps part of a plan (as Henry Kissinger later surmised) "to keep us from using atomic weapons or from bombing Chinese territory," as well as possibly to forestall in advance any possible American use of the weapons in question.[34]

What in retrospect stands out about the history of official deception and lies in this wretched "germ warfare" story is the gullibility of scientists on both sides. The case against the United States was dismissed out of hand in 1952 by Sir Macfarlane Burnet (a 1960 Nobel Prize–winner for his work in virology) because such acts made neither military nor scientific sense and it was "unthinkable" that any government would have authorized them.[35] Burnet made this assessment in ignorance of the actual Japanese biological experiments and campaigns in China during World War II. On the other hand, the British biochemist Needham decided that the charges against the United States must be true because he had studied Japanese wartime record and he did not believe his Chinese colleagues capable of lies and conspiracy. In both cases, distinguished scientists were swayed by moral considerations to reach unscientific and unsound conclusions.

### "CONVENTIONAL" WAR

As it turned out, "conventional" weapons were quite capable of exacting almost as terrible a toll as weapons of mass destruction. Napalm was, for instance, employed on a massive scale; 7.8 million gallons (35.4 million liters) were used in just the first three months of the war. In London, Prime Minster Winston Churchill protested without avail to his advisers about "splashing it about all over the civilian population,"[36] and some allied pilots expressed shock at having "killed civilians, friendly civilians, and bombed their homes; fired whole villages with their occupants."[37] Late in 1950, MacArthur gave orders for "every means of communication, every installation, factory, city and village" in North Korea to be destroyed.[38] The country was to be turned into, in the words of historian Bruce Cumings, "a wilderness of scorched earth."[39] And this was done. For much of the three-year-long war, the United States held almost complete dominance of North Korean skies. The intensity of bombing was such that much of the population had to spend daylight hours quite literally underground. General Curtis LeMay, planner of the U.S. Air Force's saturation bombing campaigns that destroyed nearly every significant city in Japan in 1945, now turned his attention to Korea. He boasted later that "over a period of three years or so, we burned down just about every town in North and South Korea both . . . we killed off over a million civilian Koreans and drove several million more from their homes."[40] Attacks on the fabric of civil society also included a 500 bomber raid in June 1952 that destroyed a complex of hydroelectric power stations on the Yalu River, knocking out 90 percent of the country's remaining power supply;[41] massive air assaults in July and August 1952 on Pyongyang, the heaviest bombing attack to that date on a capital,[42] which drenched the city in napalm and produced a civilian death toll of 6,000; and finally, in May 1953, the bombing of the irrigation dams on which the agricultural infrastructure of the country depended.[43] That raid was designed to starve the enemy into submission.

The forces of the United Nations quite literally devastated the country, exacting a biblical toll. For much of the country, not a stone was left upon a stone. An overwhelming proportion of the war's three to four million casualties were civilian (as Curtis Le May seemed proud to declare). The Northern side, whatever its moral qualities, simply did not have the capacity to mete out indiscriminate death to the civilian population by bombing, strafing, napalming, blasting dams, or destroying food crops.

Civil wars excite bitter passions notoriously difficult to contain in structured and disciplined military activity. The Geneva Conventions were little honored in Korea. The fact that Seoul was repeatedly "liberated" by both sides in the Korean War meant that those seen by the "liberating" force at any time as having collaborated with the preceding occupation were liable to be rooted out and punished.

At the outbreak of war in 1950, one of the first acts of the Rhee regime was to order the execution of political prisoners, whose deaths were in due course attributed to atrocities by the incoming Northern forces.[44] In Seoul, there was only time to execute "about a hundred communists" (according to an Australian diplomatic source), but elsewhere many more were killed. Declassified U.S. documents indicated that "more than 2,000" political prisoners were executed without trial in these early weeks; hundreds of them were taken out to sea from the port of Pohang and shot, their bodies dumped overboard. U.S. Ambassador John Muccio urged the South Korean authorities to carry out executions only after "due process" and "in a humane manner," but he did not press his point.[45] Throughout the country, according to Gregory Henderson, then a U.S. Embassy official in Seoul and later a prominent historian of Korea, probably over 100,000 people were killed without trial or legal warrant.[46] Investigations into all this have scarcely begun, and the overwhelming impression, part of the propaganda of wartime, that the North alone was brutal and inhuman remains unshaken.

Yet the Northern occupation began with the opening of Seoul's central jail and the release of all political prisoners who had survived because there had not been enough time to shoot them. The North's occupation of Seoul and much of the rest of South Korea lasted only about two months. Although the process of "liberation" by an army representing a sharply contrasting set of values was inevitably traumatic, General William Dean, commander of the American forces at the battle of Taejon, who spent several weeks cut off from his command before being captured, remarked later, "To me, the civilian attitude [toward the KPA] seemed to vary between enthusiasm and passive acceptance."[47] An Air Force study of the occupation of Seoul noted that it was a time of "music, theatre, parades, huge spectacles," during which the invaders "in general were not ruthless." A simple program was propounded of "a united and free Korea, and redistribution and nationalization of industry, equal status for women, a broad program of social betterment, lower prices and an assured living for workers, and more efficient and honest government." While the "masses" did not rise up with spontaneous enthusiasm to welcome the KPA, despite the claims to the contrary by Kim Il Sung's propagandists, there was little doubt that many people approved its program.[48] The restoration of the People's Committees and the implementation of land reform were also popular.[49] Youth were forcibly impressed into the Northern forces, and executions did occur, especially as collapse became imminent. The worst incidents evidently occurred as the North Koreans were pulling back quickly in the face of the advances of General MacArthur's forces following the Inchon landings.[50] A recent study suggests that 1,800 prisoners from the jails of Pyongyang and 500 from Wonsan might have been summarily executed as the retreat took place.[51]

The overall picture adds up to nothing pretty, but something less than "bestiality," the term chosen by the authors of an Air Force report to characterize it. The major American study of the matter concludes that:

There is no evidence that such acts of barbarism against UN soldiers were ever countenanced by NKPA [North

Korean People's Army] commanders—in fact, orders were issued by the General Headquarters of the North Korean Army to prevent the unnecessary slaughter of prisoners of war.[52]

When Seoul was recaptured by U.S. and South Korean forces, perhaps as many as 29,000 Koreans were executed on suspicion of collaboration with the North.[53] As the allied forces proceeded north, a similar pattern evolved. The occupation of Pyongyang and many other cities and villages above the 38th parallel was characterized by atrocities. While there is no agreed-upon figure for the number of those killed during this phase of the "liberation" of North Korea from communist rule, internal U.S. intelligence reports describe "a nauseating reign of terror"[54] in line with a policy to "root out and destroy communists and collaborators."[55] According to one estimate, 150,000 people were executed or kidnapped.[56]

The official U.S. Army report at the end of the war gave 7,334 as the figure for civilian victims of North Korean atrocities, a small fraction of those now known to have been executed by Rhee in the first moments of the war alone.[57] This figure was scarcely consistent with the estimate of the deaths of 5,000 to 7,500 civilians attributed to a single incident, known as the Taejon Massacre. This incident, described as "worthy of being recorded in the annals of history along with the Rape of Nanking, the Warsaw Ghetto, and other similar mass exterminations," became the centerpiece of the U.S. case for North Korean brutality. A U.S. Army report on the massacre, including graphic photographs, was published around the world in October 1953.[58] The notion of North Korea as fanatical and brutal owes much to the way the violence of the Korean War was communicated to the world a half century ago.

At Taejon, a town about 160 kilometers south of Seoul, a massacre undoubtedly occurred. The first published references to it appeared in the North Korean newspaper *Choson Inminbo*, referring to a massacre of around 7,000 people, including many former pro–North Korean partisans held in Taejon prison, which reportedly took place over about five days in early July, 1950. Up to eighty trucks each day were used to cart prisoners to a village where they were either doused with gasoline and burned to death or dumped in air-defense trenches and killed.[59] Alan Winnington, correspondent for the *Daily Worker*, the English communist paper, accompanying the (North) Korean People's Army on their march southward, reported having inspected mass graves at a village called Rangwul near Taejon. He concluded from inspection of the graves, photographic evidence, and discussions with villagers in the vicinity that approximately 7,000 prisoners from the jails of Taejon and nearby had been summarily executed at that spot and buried in mass graves dug by locally press-ganged peasants.

The two Australian officers who constituted the UNCOK Field Observer team, Major Peach and Wing Commander Rankin, were in the Taejon area just when Winnington concluded a massacre must have taken place, acting as liaison officers between the UN and South Korean forces. On July 9, they were, Peach wrote, on the "road from Taejon to Konju"[60] when they saw trucks loaded with prisoners going south. As Peach recalled in a 1982 interview with this author, "Before my very eyes I saw at least two or three killed, their heads broken like eggs with the butts of rifles."[61]

Later, in Konju, they were told that prisoners were being shot.[62] A contemporary photograph in the London *Picture Post* shows a truckload of such prisoners, described as "South Korean suspected traitors," on the banks of the Kum River "on their way to execution."[63] Four days later, on July 13, the Northern forces crossed the Kum River, and on July 20 captured Taejon, which was still burning when Winnington reached it. The sequence of events strongly suggests that Winnington, Peach, and Rankin were all witnesses to different stages of the same terrible event.

There was one further witness. Philip Deane, the captured correspondent for the London *Observer*, was told a story while in a prison camp in North Korea of a massacre in Taejon just before the town fell to the communists. His informant was a French priest. Deane wrote:

> [Father Cadars] told me that just before the Americans retreated from the town, South Korean police had brought into a forest clearing near his church 1,700 men, loaded layer upon layer into trucks. These prisoners were ordered out and ordered to dig long trenches. Father Cadars watched. Some American officers, Cadars said were also watching. When a certain amount of digging was complete, South Korean policemen shot half the prisoners in the back of the neck. The other half were then ordered to bury the dead.[64]

After Father Cadars's protest was dismissed, the remainder were likewise killed. He was told they were "Communist guerrillas who rebelled in the Taejon gaol."

Unless, by some terrible version of serendipity, there were two massacres in the Taejon vicinity, it is hard to avoid the conclusion that the most brutal North Korean atrocity in the South was actually a Southern atrocity in a brutal ongoing civil war.

This version of the Taejon massacre was also reported by the military *attaché* to the U.S. embassy, Lt. Colonel Bob E. Edwards, who sent a report together with photographs on to U.S. intelligence in Washington. The figure of 1,800 massacre victims was given, but South Korean forces were clearly blamed, and the orders to execute the prisoners were described as having come from "the highest authority."[65] Some time between then and 1953, somebody—presumably in either the

American military or government—seems to have made the decision to turn this into a Northern massacre, the characteristic, single atrocity of the entire war. The truth seems inescapable: This worst atrocity of the war was committed by forces acting in the name of the United Nations, and a concerted effort was then made to cover it up by blaming it on the North Korean enemy.

In 1992, more than forty years after the events occurred, in a South Korean monthly journal, men who had actually taken part in the massacre confirmed Winnington's account, though not the numbers he suggested.[66] The only matter which remained unclear was whether Americans had been directly involved or not.

A much smaller incident, in which according to South Korean records 248 civilians were killed, wounded, or missing following an attack when seeking refuge in a railway tunnel at a place called Nogunri in the week following Taejon incident, became the subject of international attention following publication of an Associated Press investigation in September 1999.[67] The U.S. Army then conducted a full investigation, concluding that the deaths were the regrettable result of confusion on the part of poorly trained, raw American soldiers. In January 2001, President Clinton expressed regret, but not an apology, for what had happened.[68] The great massacre at Taejon went unmentioned.

### ENDING THE WAR

The initial UN commitment in June 1950 was to repel aggression by driving the invading forces back where they came from. But the underlying problem from which the war stemmed was that of Korean nationalism, resistance to an American-imposed division of the peninsula and a deep desire to unify the nation. That was the cause for which both sides fought. The UN did not stop at the 38th parallel heading northward, nor did the

Chinese–North Korean forces stop there on their southward march. Yet, with the UN and China both committed, the best to be hoped for was a negotiated settlement, the alternative being an actual global war, probably involving nuclear weapons.

In March 1951, a UN counteroffensive forced the Northern forces to give up Seoul a second time. By then its population had dropped from 1.5 million to 200,000, its water supply had collapsed, and illness was rife. Thereafter the war entered a phase of stalemate and attrition, with huge armies, more or less evenly balanced on the ground, seesawing back and forth across a relatively narrow band of territory in the general vicinity of where the war had begun but with the United Nations side in virtually total control of the air and the sea, and so pounding North Korea mercilessly. In July 1951, talks toward a settlement opened in the town of Kaesong, about seventy kilometers north of Seoul. The North Korean delegate, Li Sang-Jo, remarked later that his side expected the talks to last a few days.[69] They would actually continue for another two years.

The first problem was where to draw the new line—on the 38th parallel again, or on the "actual line of contact on the battlefield," which was difficult to define since much of the territory was contested. Initially the understanding was that the line would simply be at the parallel again, but the United States refused that, "as a matter of major principle," and began a new push northward,[70] attempting to persuade the enemy to cede territory in return for a U.S.–UN agreement to refrain from exploiting its air and naval supremacy. In the meantime, an international campaign was launched to tar the other side as the perpetrators of atrocities as well as fanatical, unreasonable negotiators.

After nuclear intimidation, sustained bombardment from sea and air, and some of the fiercest land battles of the entire war, the stalled talks resumed on October 25, 1951, at Panmumjon. But this time, with the 38th parallel more or less agreed upon as the line, a new bone of contention emerged: how to deal with the repatriation of large numbers of prisoners of war captured by both sides. The communist side proposed the implementation of the 1949 Geneva Convention (Article 198), which called for immediate and total repatriation of all prisoners upon cessation of hostilities, but the United States countered with a new principle: "voluntary repatriation." This was at least in part based on the humanitarian grounds that any prisoner should in the end have the freedom to choose where and to whom he wanted to be released, but it was equally designed to inflict a propaganda defeat on the other side by demonstrating that, given a choice, many of the prisoners in UN hands would refuse repatriation to "tyranny."[71] The chief U.S.–UN negotiator at Panmunjom, Admiral C. Turner Joy, later wrote:

It was thought that if any substantial portion of the ex-Communist soldiers refused to return to communism, a huge setback to Communist subversive activities would ensue. I regret to say this does not seem to have been a valid point.[72]

The war, however, dragged on for another two years on the basis of this principle, during which the United Nations side suffered 140,000 casualties, including 9,000 American dead, and about half a million more civilian Koreans died. Within the camps, the determination to gain a propaganda victory on both sides led to the imposition of a reign of terror and brutality. On the admission of General Ridgway's Head Office, more POWs died in United Nations camps than in North Korean camps, however bad conditions were in the latter.[73] One reason was that control in the camps was largely given to

South Korean or Chinese (Nationalist) guards. Those prisoners who expressed a wish to return home were tattooed with anti-communist slogans and "either beaten black and blue or killed," according to Admiral Joy.[74] When a series of rebellions then occurred in the UN-run POW camps, they were put down with tanks and flame-throwers; 334 prisoners died in the process.[75]

Ultimately, of the total of over 98,000 prisoners held in UN hands, 22,604 prisoners were handed over to an international custodial force rather than repatriated to North Korea or China.[76] Two out of three Chinese prisoners chose to go to Taiwan rather than return to China, not such a foolish decision since many of those who actually chose to be returned to China were subsequently punished for "collaboration" with the enemy.[77] But the outcome was far from being a propaganda triumph. Among Korean prisoners in Northern camps, one in five of those whose homes were in the South chose to stay behind, and to the eternal shock of the Americans, twenty-one American POWs chose to go to China instead of returning to the United States.[78] There had, of course, been little of the atmosphere necessary to make a free choice in any of the camps, and the December 1953 report of the Neutral Nations Repatriation Committee concluded: "[A]ny prisoner who desired repatriation had to do so clandestinely and in fear of his life."[79] The experience of captivity under such conditions so overwhelmed some of the prisoners that they refused to have anything to do with either South or North Korea afterward, preferring instead to go into exile in India, or even Brazil.

The counterpart of the reign of terror that "voluntary repatriation" brought to the UN prisoner camps in the South was an intense propaganda campaign to establish that camps in the North were far worse. In November 1951, the judge-advocate of the U.S. 8th Army, Colonel James Hanley, declared that over

5,500 prisoners, most of them presumably American, had been massacred in those camps since the war began. Through the war as a whole, approximately 2,700 American prisoners died in captivity, which means they died of cold, hunger, illness, or ill-treatment, but the number of POWs whose death as a result of "atrocities" could be confirmed was subsequently revised to 365.[80] In UN camps, on the other hand, the casualty rate among Chinese and North Korean prisoners was far greater: 6,600 of them died while in UN hands just to the end of 1951.[81]

Allegations of brainwashing prisoners, particularly of U.S. pilots who "confessed" to taking part in bacteriological warfare bombing raids, were also widely circulated. In general, however, the worst atrocities—especially the murder or ill-treatment of prisoners—tended to occur during the chaotic conditions of 1950–51. Later, official studies of this problem concluded, as did the Australian Army, that there was no evidence of torture or atrocities to Australian prisoners.[82] Britain's (former) chief of the Defence Staff, Lord Carver, agreed that "The UN prisoners in Chinese hands . . . were certainly much better off in every way than any held by the Americans."[83]

Further factors that delayed a peace settlement were the refusal of Syngman Rhee's government to countenance an end to the war on any terms other than victory and the use of terror and intimidation by the regime to maintain Rhee's power. As conspiracy trials ground on in the courts and mobs surrounded the National Assembly to ensure passage of the constitutional "reforms" necessary for Rhee to retain power, U.S. authorities agonized over plans to organize their own coup to overthrow him.[84] General Mark Clark, commander of the UN forces, called Rhee "as unscrupulous a dictator as ever lived."[85]

Eventually, though, Rhee survived, the "voluntary" principle was accepted, POWs were exchanged, and a cease-fire was signed on July 27, 1953, after just over three years and one month of fighting. In "Operation Big Switch," the UN Command handed over 12,773 prisoners to the other side and 359 to the Indian custodial forces, while the North Korean–Chinese side returned 75,801 prisoners to the UN Command and 22,604 to the Indian custodial forces.[86] The cease-fire, signed by China, North Korea, and the United States (but not South Korea), still remains to be converted into a permanent peace settlement. If there was no victor, there were countless victims—relatively more in North Korea as a percentage of population than in the Soviet Union at the end of the Second World War. The generation that survived still struggles with the physical and psychological scars of war, and the problem that gave rise to the war in the first place—national division—remains unresolved. It remains, in fact, modern Korea's original sin.

## Never Again

It is sobering to look back at these events in the light of the intervening half-century. America's Korea policy, subject to the overarching imperative of anticommunism, was implacably opposed to self-determination, a goal that ultimately requires reunification. In 2003, while many commentators looked to the U.S. occupation of Japan for lessons and precedents that might guide a similar process after the war in Iraq, nobody considered the far more apt Korea precedent. While the occupation of the former enemy, Japan, was seen as benevolent and experienced as liberating, enjoying as it did the cooperation even of the Japanese Communist Party and accomplishing a transition to democracy, the occupation of Korea was the reverse: division, followed by repression and terror. The one was as repressive as the other was enlightened. The one is positively, even fondly remembered by many Japanese and much of the world; the other is studiously forgotten, except by Koreans, South and North, who tasted its bitter fruits.

To enforce and institutionalize the division of the peninsula, democrats and nationalists were crushed and international legitimacy extracted by pressure, threat, deception, and manipulation from a deeply reluctant United Nations. As two rival states emerged, both committed to Korean national unity, conflict became inevitable. When the war broke out in June 1950, one side was communist and the other anticommunist, but neither was democratic.

The UN entry into the war was of questionable legitimacy. If the war was indeed a civil war, the intervention should have lain beyond its powers, but at the time many assumed that North Korea was simply a Soviet puppet and that Stalin was launching a bid for global dominance. It is true that when Kim Il Sung launched the war he was dependent on the Soviet Union economically, militarily, and politically, and he could not have acted without Stalin's blessing. Kim, however, persuaded a reluctant Stalin to support his bid for a resolution of the problem of Korean division, not vice versa. A "coalition of the willing" was mobilized under the UN standard but U.S. command. Japan, still under American occupation and with the ink scarcely dry on its pacifist constitution, was persuaded to dispatch a mine clearing unit in conditions of maximum secrecy. The UN forces flouted the rules of war by allowing or encouraging South Korean forces to engage in widespread massacres and torture, the details of which are as yet only slowly being revealed. The United States itself committed a series of war crimes, only partially acknowledged and never in any way expiated, by attacking civilian population centers, refugee columns, and the North's civil infrastructure including dams and food supplies (crimes for which German officers had been executed only a few years before); introduced "brainwashing" practices on a large scale in the POW camps under its command—while accusing the Chinese of doing precisely the same thing—thereby prolonging the war significantly and increasing greatly its casualties; and came very close to the use of nuclear weapons (on which it then had a virtual monopoly).

As the Korean historian Park Myung-lim notes, the United States fought a total war, deeming legitimate the use of any and all means that seemed likely to achieve its objective of military victory. North Korea fought with all its means, but these were clearly no match in destructive power, even with large-scale Chinese and Russian military aid. As for Stalin, he was careful at all costs to avoid Soviet involvement and was prepared, if need be, to cut his losses and write North Korea off altogether.[87] Between three and four million people died, most of them Korean civilians, and ten million were cut off from their families on either side of the cease-fire line. In proportional terms, North Korea suffered greater losses of population than either the Soviet Union or Poland in the Second World War. The American losses were long put at 54,000 men, almost as many as would die during the decade-long Vietnam War, but in 2000 these figures were mysteriously scaled back to 36,940, with the explanation that by a clerical error all U.S. military deaths during those years had been counted as Korean War deaths.[88]

It is a grim record, but nothing is so grim as the fact that so little of it is recorded in the popular memory. Instead, the war is remembered as constructed at the time—as purely a manifestation of North Korean aggressiveness, criminality, and brutality. To know in even the most summary form the horrors and the futility of the actual experience is to understand how abhorrent is the thought that such a war could ever be contemplated again.

Whatever the Northern regime might have become without the war we can only speculate. What it was to become in the wake of one of the most devastating wars of the twentieth century was a country uniquely obsessed with survival, imbued with the spirit of unity, leadership, and sacrifice. The state of permanent emergency and mobilization that has lasted now for over half a century can only be relaxed when the temporary cease-fire is converted into a permanent peace.

# THE JUCHE WORLD: FATHER, SON, AND STATE

The "North Korea" problem today captures headlines and vexes governments, think-tanks, and peoples around the world, yet only two North Korean names are widely recognized: Kim Il Sung and Kim Jong Il, father and son. This is not surprising, given that the North Korean media scarcely ever refers to any other individuals and the state is commonly equated with its leader and his family. The country whose official name is "Democratic People's Republic of Korea" is in reality neither democratic nor republican, but an absolute monarchy. It would be no exaggeration for its ruler to utter, as could no other contemporary world leader, the famous words attributed to Louis XIV, "I am the state."

Its first leader, Kim Il Sung, was born in 1912 and died in 1994, but a 1998 constitutional revision reserved the post of president for him "eternally." Time, by a 1997 edict, is dated from his birth, so that 2004 is the year 92 on the North Korean calendar. After his father's death, Kim Jong Il took over the reins of the country and holds them to this day. The presidency being permanently occupied, his official post, under which he presides over the state and receives visiting dignitaries, is chairman of the National Defense Commission.

North Korea's insistence on having a deceased person as president points both to the peculiarity of its political practice and to the huge shadow the late Kim Il Sung still casts over his country, nearly a century after his birth and ten years after his death. In ruling the country between them almost sixty years, since 1946, the Kims, father and son, establish a sort of record. In modern times only the Chiang family in (Nationalist) China and Taiwan, a father and son who ruled successively for forty-one years, came close, but the Chiangs only represented the Chinese nationalist state and ideology, they didn't build it. In North Korea, the two Kims between them have dominated the state to a degree unknown elsewhere. *Juche*, the national ideology, invented by Kim *père* and developed by Kim *fils*, is their unique legacy. Any understanding of the country today has to start from these two men and their idea.

Many myths have been spread about Kim Il Sung, both by his believers and his detractors, but the main details of his life are now clear. The North Korean stories about how he founded a "Down with Imperialism Union" as a fourteen-year-old schoolboy and a "Korean People's Revolutionary Army" in 1934, or about holding out throughout the war in the mountainous northeast corner of Korea before finally triumphing over Japan in August 1945, are complete fabrications. He was indeed a prominent anti-fascist fighter in the 1930s, but his credentials were complex and internationalist rather than "purely" Korean. Born Kim Song-Ju in Pyongyang in 1912, he left Korea for neighboring Manchuria (northeast China) as a child of seven with his parents, who were escaping the oppression of Japanese colonialism. In 1931, he joined the Chinese Communist Party and was described in a December 1935 report to the Comintern as "trusted and respected" both by his men and the command of anti-Japanese guerrilla units.[1] In June 1937, he led his unit (comprising many Koreans) across the border in a widely reported raid on Japanese positions in the Korean town of Pochombo. He was then operating as part of the North-Eastern Anti-Japanese United Army, a Chinese unit in a Chinese force.[2] When the special Japanese Maeda Unit was organized and sent to root out his guerrilla band, Kim led a counterattack in February 1940 that killed 120 of its 145 men. From then on, he was hated (and feared) by the Japanese. On their October 1940 "wanted" list, he is known as "the tiger" (*tora*). Other guerrilla leaders were labeled "bear," "lion," "bull," "roe deer," "cat," and "horse." Late in that year, as Japanese repression intensified, he retreated to the Soviet Union, where, until the war ended, he served as a captain in the Red Army's 88th Special Brigade.

When the war ended he returned to Korea on a Soviet ship, the *Pugacheff*, landing at Wonsan on September 19, 1945. With him, either on the same ship or soon after, were 105 of his comrades from the Manchurian anti-Japanese resistance movement, and it was this group on which the North Korean state was then built. Representing himself as the faithful instrument of Soviet policy, fulsome in his praise of Stalin, the Red Army, and the Soviet Union, and relatively young and energetic, Kim Il Sung readily won favor with the occupying forces. The preferred leader among Soviet, Chinese, and Korean forces, he was, according to the CIA, "conceded by all circles to have vast popular prestige."[3] His leadership was confirmed by Stalin in August 1946.

From 1948 to 1972, North Korea was officially a "People's Democracy" and thereafter (by its constitution) a "socialist" state, characterized (in Leninist terms) by the dictatorship of the party. From Stalin, or more broadly from his Chinese and Soviet communist experience, Kim learned the importance of organization. The North Korean Workers Party became a centralized party of iron discipline and Kim Il Sung gradually purged one after another of its factions other than his own— those 100-odd Manchurian comrades who were with him through thick and thin, until he was in unquestioned control of party, state, and army. On the surface, the country was a communist state, like the Soviet Union or the satellite states of eastern Europe, in which a dictatorship in the name of the proletariat was implemented by the communist party. Behind the formal and nominally democratic institutions of state stood the politburo, the ultimate repository of power, and behind that stood the Central Committee of the Communist Party of the Soviet Union. Behind, or above, that stood Joseph Stalin, until his death in 1953, the unquestioned monarch of the communist world.

To maintain his regime against the threats of internal division and external aggression, Kim paid attention as much to social control as to defense preparation.[4] His rule was marked by periodic purges, spying, and ruthless suppression of dissent, intense and sustained propaganda, and control of information. The public security apparatus, in effect the secret police, was closely supervised by Kim in person as it spread its tentacles throughout the society, with informants and agents maintaining a regular flow of detailed information on people's thoughts and movements. The population was divided into categories of reliability and subjected to intense campaigns of ideological molding. His authority as ruler was soon represented as legitimate because it stemmed from those quite traditional values of virtue and benevolence, and clear signs of the "Cult of Kim Il Sung"—songs, poems, films to his glory—were apparent within a few years of his return to Pyongyang.[5] After the death of Stalin in 1953, this incipient cult could develop without the inhibition of subordination to any superior. To unite and inspire the people, and to consolidate and enhance his own power, he was given various roles beyond the merely constitutional head of state, as "just ruler" and "loving father" of the nation and (from the late 1960s) as *Suryong* or Great Leader. To resist or doubt his leadership or to lack enthusiasm in singing panegyrics to him as the fount of true wisdom was to court denunciation and purge. State and leader were indistinguishable. He became known at various times as Wise Creator and Builder, Genius of Thought, Lodestar of Our Times, Ever Victorious and Wise General, Supreme Brain of the Nation, Leader of the Third World, Hero of the twentieth-century, Sun of the World, Greatest Leader in 1000 Years, whose "tactics and strategy amaze even God."[6]

In the words of the North Korean song "We Live in the Bosom of the Leader":[7]

> *His love is boundlessly warm*
> *It is the brilliant sunshine*
> *We live in the bosom of the leader*
> *We boast of our happiness to the world*
> *Oh, our heavenly leader Marshall Kim Il Sung*
> *The people look up to him swearing allegiance.*

The personality cult aspect of the North Korean system puzzles observers. Why should this small Asian country produce arguably the most extreme form of personality (and family) cult known to modern history? Explanations that focus exclusively on Stalinist borrowings miss the fact that it is rooted as much, if not more, in Korean tradition as in any "modern" political ideology. Korea was the most deeply Confucian of east Asian societies, and the core virtue, as taught in the "Analects" of Confucius, is filial piety (*hyo*), which takes precedence over loyalty (*chung*). Conscious of the tradition by which Korean families treasured their lineage charts, (*chok'po*), preserving the record of male descent lines from generation to generation for up to, and in some cases longer than, 1,000 years, those who constructed the North Korean state strove to represent it in terms of this primordial sense of patriarchy and family rather than simply the "modern" and more abstract bonds of state loyalty. Even in South Korea, the substitution of national loyalty for family and clan or regional ties has been a slow and far-from-complete process, and the ritual observances associated with the patriarchal lineage remain of paramount importance. The geographical isolation of traditional Korea, North and South, and its high degree of ethnic homogeneity, made it easier for both modern states to represent nation as an extended family. That sense of kinship seems to have survived remarkably intact, North and South, through fifty years of division and serves to underpin the growing dialogue about how to reunify the state, which is really about how to reunite the family.

When the Great Leader died suddenly in 1994 he was in effect the world's senior statesman, the sole surviving state leader with a record of personal participation in the anti-fascist struggle of the 1930s. He had witnessed the victory over fascism, the Cold War, the progress of glasnost and perestroika, and the collapse of the Communist Party in the Soviet Union and then of the Soviet Union itself. He had seen the toppling of dictators across eastern Europe, including many who had been his friends (and of their statues and memorials), and the rush to embrace capitalism that followed. He had seen the inroads of the market and capitalism in China and the waves of new thought that led to the Tiananmen massacre there in 1989. Perhaps most bitterly, he had witnessed a succession of economic and diplomatic triumphs by South Korea, as its trade blossomed and it made wide-ranging contacts with both China and the Soviet Union. Before he died, he seems to have realized that change in his own system was inevitable. To his son fell the task of grappling with this changed world.

By the time the final steps in his son's succession were taken, following three years of full Confucian mourning honors, Kim Jong Il had been at the helm for more than two decades, presiding over party and state. After his father's death, he simply consolidated the process. From positions already held as secretary of the Central Committee, member of the State Secretariat and the Military Commission, and commander of the armed forces, it remained only to become General Secretary of the Workers' Party in 1997. In the following year, however, he assumed a completely new position, chairman of the National Defense Commission, and from 1999 the doctrine of "Army First" politics signaled that he was in effect reconstructing the state inherited from his father. The Workers' Party continued to function at the base level as an instrument of administration and control, but the center of gravity in Kim Jong Il's state shifted from party to army. The Workers' Party has held no Congress since 1980 and its Central Committee is not known to have been convened since December 1993. North Korea today is probably better thought of as a military dictatorship than a communist state.

Officially, Kim Jong Il is said to have been born in 1942 in a guerrilla camp on the sacred Baekdu Mountain near the border with China, while his father was leading the national resistance against Japan. None of this happened. He was born in the Soviet Maritime Province military camp to which Kim Il Sung had retreated in 1940, and he arrived in Korea for the first time with his father in 1945. After graduating from Kim Il Song University in 1964, he worked in the Korean Worker's Party's organization and propaganda departments. He also developed a strong interest in the arts, writing texts on film, dance, architecture, music, and painting.

Kim Jong Il's rise may be correlated with the honorific titles bestowed upon him: Party Center (September 1973), Unique Leader (1975, when his birthday was made a national holiday), Wise and Respected Leader (1977), Dear and Beloved Leader (1980), Supreme Commander (1983), Father of the Nation and Leader of the People (August 1993), Our Father (October 1993), Dear General (1997), and subsequently Great

General, Our General, or Leader of 21st Century, Sun of the 21st Century, Glorious Sun of the 21st Century, Son of Baekdu Mountain, Sun of the Human Race and Everlasting Sky.[8] But "Dear and Beloved Leader" or simply "Dear Leader," became his most common appellation. Since his own accomplishments were in fact few, however, and bore no comparison to those of his father, his prestige rested heavily on the fact of being his father's son. As any good Confucian household would accept as natural and proper the succession of eldest son in a respected family, so Kim Jong Il's succession was represented and apparently understood by many, perhaps most, of the North Korean people.

Perhaps partly out of trepidation about his ability to fill his father's shoes, Kim Jong Il stepped up the rhetoric of the golden lineage, his father's divine genius, and their closeness. References to his own brilliance and virtue grew in extravagance. He was "superior to Christ in love, superior to Buddha in benevolence, superior to Confucius in virtue, and superior to Mohammad in justice."[9] What kind of man he really was remained long shrouded in mystery, but in recent years the veil has been at least partially lifted. Prominent figures who have spent time with him insist that he is a rational, intelligent, even (according to some) sensitive man. As more and more members of Kim Jong Il's entourage—including his former movie studio chief, his cooks (one Italian and one Japanese), one of his bodyguards, various traveling companions, and former household members—publish their memoirs (albeit thus far only in Korean and Japanese) his thoughts, foibles, and habits have been revealed in some detail.

Kim Jong Il's artistic and theatrical tastes are apparent in the monument-studded landscape whose creation he spent thirty years supervising. As he left his family mark on the physical landscape, so he helped to justify his succession. The landscape is now littered with monuments, as many as 50,000 of them by one estimate, often in marble or granite. Prominent among them are the Museum of the Korean Revolution (with 4.5 kilometers of exhibits showing the life and achievements of the leader and his family in 95 halls), museums and statues built in various locations to both parents of Kim Il Sung and sundry other relatives, a museum in the northeastern mountains that houses the 28,000 items presented to Kim Il Sung by foreign leaders from 146 countries, the twenty-five-meter bronze statue to him, the 170-meter Juche Tower (presumably modeled on, and slightly surpassing in height, the Washington Monument), and the sixty-meter-high Arch of Triumph (plainly modeled on, and about eleven meters higher than, the *Arc de Triomphe* in Paris), built on the occasion of Kim Il Sung's seventieth birthday in 1982 of 25,500 blocks of white granite, one for each day he had lived up until that time. The whole country, especially the capital, Pyongyang, was turned by his hand into something like a giant film set.

Kim Jong Il loves movies. His private collection of videos is said to include 20,000 mostly "pirate" versions collected by North Korean diplomatic missions, including all Academy-Award winners.[10] But, not content with watching, he also wanted to make movies to impress the world. It is hard to think of a more bizarre and unlikely venture, indicative of a curious blend of grand opera-imperial fantasy, ruthlessness, and pragmatism, than his chosen method for turning his country's film industry into a class act. In 1978, he had the renowned South Korean film director and his actress wife, Shin Sang-ok and Choi Eun-hee, abducted from Hong Kong by North Korean agents. Shin indeed subsequently directed, and Choi starred in, seven films at Pyongyang studios, which won prizes at eastern European festivals and seemed to meet Kim Jong Il's desire for international recognition. Their output also included a socialist Godzilla film, *Pulgasari*, which developed a minor cult following among film buffs outside the socialist bloc because it was (according to one enthusiast) "so terrifically bad."[11]

In their memoirs, Shin writes of spending his first five years in North Korea in detention. He made several failed escape attempts before making his peace with Kim Jong Il in 1983. "Pardoned," he was allowed to set up "Shin Films" studio.[12] Given a substantial budget, Shin and Choi thereafter traveled frequently to eastern Europe, from which, in 1986, they sought refuge in the American embassy in Vienna. When they fled, Shin took the sum of $2.2 million from a Bank of America account in Vienna; Pyongyang sued, insisting the money was meant for a film on Genghis Khan. To the allegations of theft, Shin responded that the money was compensation for abduction and detention, and the suit seems to have been dropped. Much later, as chair of the jury of the 2001 International Film Festival at Pusan, in South Korea, Shin looked back on a career in Seoul, Pyongyang, and Hollywood and remarked that he thought his best film was one made during his Pyongyang years, *Runaway*, which dealt with a wandering Korean family in 1920s Manchuria. Ironically, *Runaway* was withdrawn from screening at the Festival by order of the South Korean Supreme Prosecutor.[13] Whether North or South, Shin seemed destined to spend his life struggling with the authorities.

The Shin-Choi memoirs provide a valuable, if unflattering, insight into Kim Jong Il's mind. They present him as a pampered young aristocrat, accustomed to a sybaritic lifestyle in a chain of villas scattered throughout the country equipped with saunas and elaborate video facilities. He had, they write, a complex about his shortness, wearing high-heeled boots and describing himself to Choi self-deprecatingly as "Little Fatso."[14] The Kim regime had many of the qualities of a feudal court. Loyalty to Kim Jong Il, the royal route to power and privilege, had to be constantly renewed by acts of self-denigration and pledges of fealty. On the successful completion of one project their film production company received from him a New Year's present of fifty roe deer, four hundred pheasants, two hundred geese, and two hundred cases of Japanese tangerines. The receipt of the gift was the occasion among the employees for weeping, dancing, celebration, and, most importantly, the renewal of loyalty pledges.[15]

Shin loathed Kim Jong Il, but found him a formidable figure, remarking, "[H]e has eyes that see reality, is no fool, and reads the hearts of flatterers."[16] Since Shin's story was published, many others have refuted our media's representation of the North Korean leader as simply a vain, incompetent, and foolish fanatic. Other accounts, however, offer different perspectives. A senior Russian official who spent twenty-four days traveling across Russia by train with Kim in 2001 referred to his "strong personal energy" and "powerful aura."[17] He found Kim to be steeped in classical Chinese thought and in the politics and history of the modern world, a knowledgeable, multifaceted, adroit man as well as a gourmand and *bon vivant*. On the train journey, Kim took with him a special team of chefs who prepared meals to Korean, Russian, Japanese, Chinese, or French cuisine, made up to fifteen to twenty dishes daily, with fresh ingredients flown from Pyongyang to intermediate stations along his route.[18] He told his traveling companion, Pulikovsky, that he had given up heavy drinking, confining himself now to a half bottle each day of Bordeaux or Burgundy, and had stopped smoking in 1999. Kim's former Japanese chef describes banquets that began at midnight and lasted up to four days. Kim favored "the most exotic sushis" and developed an "appetite for gourmet shark fin soup three or four times a week."[19]

South Korean president Kim Dae Jung spent eleven hours in talks with him during the South-North summit meeting in 2000 and found him "a serious person with whom we can talk." That meeting gave Kim Dae Jung confidence that henceforth there would be no possibility of war on the peninsula. This sentiment was apparently widely shared in South Korea, where people who saw Kim Jong Il in a positive light suddenly jumped from 4.7 to 53.8 percent of the population, while those who saw him just as a "dictator" fell from 34.6 to 9.6 percent.[20] When Madeleine Albright, U.S. secretary of state, visited him on behalf of President Clinton later in the same year, Kim seems to have gone out of his way to be charming to her. She described her host as "serious and authoritative."

Drawing on Russian as well as Korean sources to develop a psychological profile of Kim Jong Il, Alexandre Mansourov, a Russian-born Korea specialist now working in Honolulu, concludes that Kim is "an extrovert and an internationalist by his outlook. Not only is he a man of 'modern views' who appreciates modernity, but also a man 'one can do business with,' as the Russian President Putin called him." Mansourov calls him "a strategic chess player, not a fleeting gambler," a "tough negotiator and survivor," and most importantly, in view of his supposed willingness to lead the Koreas into a new war, Mansourov reminds us, "In his war-scarred childhood, he saw pain, blood, and death close and personal. Kim Jong Il likely hates war and is very cautious not to plunge his country again into the sort of abyss he knew in his childhood."[21]

Kim's sister-in-law, Sung Hae Rang, who lived in his household from 1974 to 1996, offers an intimate and perceptive personal portrait of him in her memoirs. She describes him as a man of artistic temperament and considerable intellect, surrounded by power and luxury and deprived of the love and care of his mother, who died when Kim was seven years old. She notes sadly that he therefore grew up without proper education or care, able to indulge his instincts without restraint. Temperamentally, he is inclined to capriciousness and volatility, but his arrogance, cruelty, and obstreperousness are tempered by innate qualities of generosity, kindness, and a desire to do good to others.[22] She sees him as a compassionate, if somewhat twisted man.

In a family state, succession is always the subject of palace intrigue and struggle. In 2002, as Kim Jong Il reached the age of 60, the same age at which his father had settled his own succession, the question of who should succeed him focused attention. Kim Jong Il's family life has been complicated. He has never had an official "consort" or wife, but his children were born to four different mothers, while his dalliances with various dancers, entertainers, and actresses are said to have been legion. His eldest son, Kim Jong-nam, born in 1971, like his father, grew up surrounded by the perquisites of absolute wealth and power but without the attentions of a mother (who took ill shortly after his birth and spent much of her time thereafter in Moscow hospitals, where she died in 2002). As a child in Pyongyang he lived a reclusive life, not attending any school at all and then, in the 1980s, was sent off to the International School in Geneva and the French school in Moscow, without ever, it seems, being anything like a dedicated student.[23]

His aunt who cared for him during those years sadly observed him turning into a playboy. Until 2001 he was nevertheless considered a likely successor. In May of that year, however, he fell from favor after being detained and held briefly at the Tokyo Detention Center for traveling on a forged Dominican passport. His explanation was that he was on a family outing to Tokyo's Disneyland with his wife and son.[24] Japanese scuttlebutt suggested Kim Jong-won was a well-known customer in Tokyo's "soapland" or sex-parlor establishments.[25] His younger brother, Kim Jong-chol, is now said to be favored for succession, with moves underway to elevate his mother, Ko Yong-hee, former primadonna of the Pyongyang Mansudae Theater and the Japan-born daughter of a well-known Japanese professional wrestler (ring-name: Daidozan

Matamichi) who migrated to North Korea around 1960, to the status of "Mother of Korea."[26]

## STATE AND IDEOLOGY

All new states must construct a tradition and moral frame that will confer legitimacy and justify control, and in North Korea Kim Il Sung based his regime at its inception on the twin pillars of resistance to Japan (Korean nationalism) and a commitment to social reform (communism under Soviet guidance). Over time, however, the former swallowed the latter; Kim shed his internationalism and his communism and became the quintessential Korean nationalist. Between them, father and son wrought the transition from a Marxist-Leninist to a unique, postcommunist ideology, to which the name *Juche*, occasionally "Kimilsungism" or "Kim Il Sung Thought," was applied. It became the exclusive ideology of the North Korean state, gradually supplanting Marxism-Leninism and being enshrined in Article 4 of the 1972 constitution as "a creative application of Marxism-Leninism" by which the state was to be "guided."[27] During the 1970s, students at Kim Il Sung University, the country's premier institution of higher learning, were spending 65 percent of their class hours studying the principles of *Juche* and the ideas of the Great Leader.[28] What to his father, Kim Il Sung, was a rhetorical tendency became under Kim Jong Il a fully-fledged system of thought, the sole state ideology.

The principal aide to whom they turned for professional, philosophical advice on how to go about this was a man named Hwang Jang Yop. Hwang studied philosophy at Tokyo's Chuo University in Japanese colonial times (1942-44) and at Moscow University after the war. As his services to the North Korean regime were recognized, he rose rapidly through the North Korean elite. When this author met him in Pyongyang in 1980 he was, among other things, president of the Supreme People's Assembly. Although six years have now passed since his defection to South Korea in 1997, the precise nature of his contribution to *Juche* thought and of his differences with the regime that led to his defection still remain to be clarified. Amid the high levels of tension between Pyongyang and Washington today, there is some irony in the fact that a red carpet was rolled out for Hwang for his October 2003 visit to Washington, where he roundly denounced his former masters.

*Juche*, literally "subject" as in "subjectivity," has complex associations but implies above all independence, the autonomy of the state, economy, and military. In terms of national posture, the very word itself established a certain distance between North Korea and its two communist neighbors, the Soviet Union and China. Koreans deemed too close to either have at various times been purged, imprisoned, and executed. The idea of a self-reliant North Korea, where the people had become the active subject of the revolutionary struggle for national survival, was meant to contrast with the dependence on foreign powers that had tragically marked earlier Korean attempts to modernize and with the presumed colonial dependency of the regime in South Korea. It was an idea that had resonance throughout Korea, South as well as North. South Korea's anticommunist, national restoration state under the autocratic former general Park Chung Hee, who ruled as president from 1961 to 1979, adopted a very similar concept, although preferring the word *chaju*, which is almost identical in meaning. Both gave priority to the idea of "self-strengthening" to achieve a "completely autonomous nation" because that was something to which Koreans had so long unsuccessfully aspired. In both North and South Korea, this notion of self-reliance (*charyok kaengseng*) was, ironically, a Korean rendering of the familiar Japanese slogan of the 1930s, *jiriki kosei*, meaning self-reliance or even autarchy. Both

North and South Korea tended to define their core ideology in those years in ways that privileged the state and its leader as the carrier of the sacred mission of national revolution and gave priority to collective over individual goals. In both could be seen more than a shadow of prewar Japanese corporatism and fascism.

*Juche* was, however, also suggestive of individual fulfillment and creativity. North Korea's classic formulation sounded like a statement of humanist principle: "Man (sic) is the master of nature and society and the main factor that decides everything." Man alone possesses *chajusong*, creativity or consciousness. In Kim Il Sung's endless and often unfathomable elaborations on *Juche*, people are called on to act "with the attitude of a master" with the mission of "transforming nature and society." As British sociologist and Korea scholar Aidan Foster-Carter observed in the 1970s, "This is surely the quintessentially Marxist theme of *homo faber*, Promethean man, whose nature it is to be perpetually transforming nature, and whose history is made of that dialectic of transformation."[29]

However, one crucial qualification was not clear in the early formulations of *Juche*. "Man," it turned out, was not only male but collective, representing in purest form the Korean nation, the historically special or chosen people destined to be the salvation of the poor and oppressed nations of the world. *Juche* in North Korea therefore came to mean both independence (from all other countries) and dependence (of everyone on the Leader).[30] It became the ideological warrant for equating absolute subservience—such that people would "think and act the way the party wants them to, anytime and anywhere"[31]— with absolute freedom of the people as "masters of the revolution"—and in this, too, could be heard distinctive echoes of past Japanese rule and in particular of the emperor-worshipping fascist state of the 1930s and 1940s.

A growing emphasis on unity, the role of the leader, and the need for ever greater effort were all characteristic of *Juche* as it developed in the hands of Kim Jong Il and Hwang Jang-yop. However, the message that "individualism" had to be overcome, since "collectivism is the fundamental demand of human beings," and that socialism required "unified guidance and control in the political, economic, cultural and all other domains of social life," demonstrated no great political or philosophical sophistication. The "absolute position of the leader in history" came to be described as a "unique, profound idea,"[32] but it was of course the basic principle both of absolute monarchs and of modern leaders such as the führer in Nazi Germany, the duce in fascist Italy, or the shah in Iran. The *Juche* world as a whole, however, drew upon many influences. Grounded in a Confucian insistence on virtue as the source of political power and patrilineal succession as the root of social stability, it incorporated the Stalinist cult of personality, familiar in all communist states but taken to unheard of heights; monarchical, hereditary family rule; a Christian stress on love and redemption; and an unusual conviction that *parousia*, or paradise, could indeed be built on earth. Within the confines of North Korea, after the collapse of the Soviet Union and more or less sealed off by the United States from contact with the outside, the construction of a unique *Juche* world could proceed under almost laboratory-like conditions.

As early as 1967, the ideological system was defined as monolithic, with the regime insisting that it possessed the absolute truth on any subject and had the right to define that truth and then to demand obedience to it. Henceforth, revealed truth would substitute for the dialectic, spirit for matter, "Kimilsungism" for Marxism—and all revelations would come directly to and through the Kims, father and son. From 1973, when he became the anointed heir to his father, Kim Jong Il had to find some way to compensate for his lack of personal charisma or of any record of service to the revolution or the state. His chosen path was to deify his father and elevate his entire family to godlike status. At his hands (and with Hwang Jang Yop's help), "Kimilsungism" and *Juche* became quasi-religious doctrines. The Korean state and its society were both modeled on the organization of the anti-Japanese partisans of the 1930s, and the term "guerrilla state" or "partisan state" became common as a characterization of North Korea.[33] Although by the end of the twentieth century most of the old Manchurian guerrilla comrades of Kim Il Sung, born between 1893 and 1925, had died, and the survivors, weighted down with medals and decorations, had been shunted aside, the myths still remained strong.[34]

Among the "Ten Principles" (in effect commandments) citizens were obliged to commit to memory, and to regularly criticize themselves and others for not fulfilling in daily life, were:[35]

1. We must give our all in the struggle to unify the entire society with the revolutionary ideology of the Great Leader Kim Il Sung.
2. We must honor the Great Leader comrade Kim Il Sung with all our loyalty.
3. We must make absolute the authority of the Great Leader comrade Kim Il Sung.

In addition to the "Ten Principles," a welter of detailed subclauses defined down to the finest detail how life was to be lived. Two of the sub-clauses under Principle Three are:

> Portraits, plaster figures, bronze statues and emblems of the respected and beloved Great Leader, publications that include the Great Leader's portrait, works of art symbolizing the Great Leader, signboards with the Great Leader's instructions, and the party's basic slogans shall all be treated with respect and protected at all costs. (Article 3.6)

> Meaningful books and relics of the history of the revo-
> lution, which are imbued with the Great Leader comrade
> Kim Il Sung's great revolutionary history and achieve-
> ments, shall be handled and maintained with respect and
> protected at all costs. (Article 3.7)

Following the mass adoption of the Mao badge in China in
about 1970, similar badges, or pins, featuring the Great Leader
were distributed in North Korea, first to officials and cadres of
some distinction, then to everyone, in a range of styles indicative of status. From 1980, everyone was obliged to wear the
badge and to treat it with the utmost respect.[36] The conferral of
the badge became an occasion for special ceremonies. The
unveiling of various formal portraits of the Leader and his
family likewise became highly ceremonial, reproducing rituals
that had surrounded the unveiling of portraits of the Japanese
emperor in colonial times. To accidentally tear, stain, or
improperly fold even a newspaper picture of a Kim, Dear or
Great, could have serious consequences. Deliberate disrespect
was almost certainly a fatal act. In place of scientific or critical
thinking, the major intellectual thrust of all Korean thinkers
thereafter became the purely theological task of elucidating the
truth as revealed in the works of the Leader. His will, rather
than the struggle between classes, became the motive force of
history.

The Great and Dear Leaders had little compunction about
imposing their wills. Periodic purges filled the concentration
camps with dissidents, suspected dissidents, and their families.
As Ogawa Haruhisa, emeritus professor of Tokyo University
and a specialist in east Asian thought, comments, "With the
establishment of the monolithic ideology in North Korea, this
unholy trinity [one-party rule, the secret police, and concentration camps] has consolidated and perpetuated itself in its cru-
elest form."[37] Among totalitarian regimes, the intensity of its

combination of terror, surveillance, and mobilization may be unmatched. Reports by United Nations sources and independent organizations such as Amnesty International paint a picture of widespread repression, with a network of camps in which somewhere between one and two hundred thousand dissidents are held, under conditions of extreme privation.[38] Prisoners "mine coal, harvest trees, manufacture goods for export and domestic consumption—from snake brandy to bicycles."[39] Defectors and refugees from North to South Korea speak of frequent beatings and a workday of fourteen to fifteen hours on a diet of corn gruel, a harsh regimen to which many prisoners succumbed.

Starting in the 1990s, survivors of the North Korean gulag began to publish their stories, and a detailed picture of it emerged. The fate of the 95,000 *Zainichi* (Japan-resident) Koreans who, between 1959 and 1970 chose to go to North Korea to participate in what they imagined to be a great experiment in building a socialist paradise, was particularly poignant. They were suspect from the start simply because of their exposure in Japan to "bourgeois" values and ideology. Many—perhaps between 10 and 20 percent—were purged and executed as the monolithic ideology and the Kim Jong Il succession were imposed in the late 1960s, while significant numbers were banished to the camps, often located in remote and dark mountain valleys; even those who escaped such ends were subject to rigorous scrutiny.[40] In the strict class frame of North Korean society, returnees were permanently locked within a "vacillating" category, insecure at the best of times.

While the "deviant" and "dissident" were confined in the dark realm of the camps, euphemistically known as the "Farm Guidance Bureau,"[41] categories of people deemed inconvenient, unnecessary, or unseemly were also removed from the bright, *Juche*-perfect center of Pyongyang. When visitors to Pyongyang, including this author in 1980, expressed curiosity at the absence of physically or mentally disabled people, it was calmly explained that in the socialist world there were no such imperfections, much less did depravities like premarital sex, divorce, prostitution, homosexuality, or drunkenness exist.[42] A recent account by a former senior official employed in North Korea's Public Security Bureau until he defected to South Korea in 1998 offers the chilling explanation that those with disabilities had been ordered out of the capital in the early 1960s, while adults of less than 150 cms in height were expelled even from rural counties. Often they were sent to remote offshore islands, forbidden to return or to reproduce.[43] Construction of the perfect world required removal of the "imperfect."

After 1986, *Juche* evolved one further stage—a new concept of the "political-social body," in which the people, the party, and the leader were linked in a triangular, or trinity-like, relationship. The "body" was assumed to have eternal life and the leader was its concentrated essence, its spirit and brain. The subjective destiny of all its individual members would only be fulfilled to the extent that the mind and will of the leader was implemented. The state now came to be represented through images familiar from fascist regimes: leader, party, and masses linked as brain (or heart), blood (or veins), and limbs (or tissue), with the role of thinking and feeling reserved, of course, for the leader, "the brain of the working masses and the center of unity and cohesion."[44] *Juche* came to embody in some near mystical and fuzzy way a fusion of "moral essence" and "bloodline" of genetic and moral superiority that could only be articulated by the "leader."[45]

That "body" image captured North Korea's unique brand of corporatism and also helped legitimize the process of succession, since only Kim Jong Il as son could truly embody the essence of the "Father President" and Great Leader. The objects of Kim's bloodline cult included not only his father but also his grandmother, grandfather, great-grandfather, great-great-grandfather, and of course mother. In his vision of succession, the pure revolutionary bloodline was insurance for the continuation of the revolution. The resulting system, though, was in essence a feudal, absolute monarchy, with a ruler who was above the law, all organs of authority—legislative, judicial, and punitive—subject to him, the entire country as his domain, state ritual celebrating only him, politics concentrated purely on the question of succession, and personal fealty as the core virtue of the regime.

The strength of the system has also been its weakness. As autonomy was sucked upward from the citizens to the leader and his retinue, initiative and creativity were destroyed, the fruits of the labor of the people consumed and wasted. Surveillance and control became the crucial focus of state energy, increasingly sapping initiative, and, since only the central leadership—the "Leader"—could be all-knowing, lateral information flows within the government and bureaucracy were deliberately constrained. Not just knowledge and power but wealth were concentrated at the core, where privilege made possible a sybaritic lifestyle.

With *Juche* as its watchword, North Korea's ultimate term of abuse was its antonym, *Sadae* (sycophant, flunkey). Yet, ironically, its efforts at home and much of its diplomatic effort abroad were devoted solely to the promotion of sycophancy and flunkeyism. For decades the purple prose that emerged from the various "seminars" and "conferences" the North Koreans organized around the world in praise of the Leader, his family, and the ineffable truths of *Juche*, like the texts of paid advertisements inserted in the world's press, were relayed back to Korea to legitimize and reinforce the cult. Vast resources were devoted to persuading the people that their leader was also a world leader, genius, hero, philosopher, and statesman. A major campaign was launched under which scholars from Russia, France, Japan, Italy, India, Bulgaria, and Tanzania, among other countries, attended international conferences solemnly devoted to celebrating the *Juche* credo that "man is the master of nature and . . . decides everything" (though the axiom that only by total subservience to the will of a leader does one attain this mastery of nature did not form part of North Korea's international agenda). The international appeal of the humanist-sounding *Juche* philosophy depended on a blind eye being turned to the absolute authority of the leader. Enthusiastic academics in Japan declared that North Korea's human-centered *Juche* philosophy opened the way to a post–Cold War world, indeed even to a post-Cartesian paradigm of knowledge.[46]

One of *Juche*'s major students (as distinct from proponents), the University of Georgia's Han S. Park, chillingly declares it to be "perhaps more coherent than any other politically engineered belief system that has ever been witnessed in history."[47] He notes that in its full flowering, there came to be not only *Juche* political theory but also *Juche* music, *Juche* architecture, *Juche* literature, *Juche* sports, and *Juche* medicine.[48] Certainly in no other industrialized, urban society has the effort to eliminate or subjugate the reflective, critical mind and to fuse the political and religious been so thoroughly pursued. Nowhere has myth been generated and propagated with such determination, "heresy" so fiercely resisted, and the very notion of the "private" so profoundly rejected.

Construction of the *Juche* world, in the physical sense, meant construction of the monumental state. Nothing better represents the essential and monumentalist *Juche* idea than the "games" at which the society celebrates and renews its identity. Adopted from fascist and communist models, under Kim Jong Il they became the central symbolic form by which the regime represented itself. Tens of thousands of students or workers become ciphers, tiny components of some patterned message or slogan, "receiving life" as single human pixels in moving patterns designed by or designed to please and satisfy the Great Leader in monumental stadiums built to celebrate, educate, and propagate the tenets of the family state. Thought and creativity are not for any of them, but for him alone. Confined to instant, reflexive obedience to his orchestrated commands, the masses celebrate and immortalize him. One consequence of a decades-long steeping of society in the *Juche* ideology is that society and state become a large-scale mass game, in which the circuits of politics, language, and economy came to be closed, controlled, and so incapable of dealing with the unexpected or unprogrammed.

The more the mythology of the *Juche* world was propagated, the more the real world suffered. As the regime shifted its priorities in the 1970s from planned economic growth and industrialization to the construction of a *Juche* world, and as the intensification of the family cult attained top priority in state affairs, the social equity and economic achievements of the 1950s and 1960s slowly eroded. Because the world of revealed truth could not tolerate either criticism or innovation, what grew in their place were bureaucratic rigidity, corruption, and rampant incompetence.

Education was subordinated to a state indoctrination so pervasive and intensive that it commenced shortly after birth. Employment assignments, food rationing, and travel constraints were all tied to a political system of comprehensive surveillance. Since institutions outside of party and state control were not allowed, there was no refuge for independent, private, or critical thought. Not only foreign travel but travel to other parts of the country was (and remains) forbidden without special permission. The regime is said to have monitored the virginity and sex lives of its female citizens by periodic compulsory physical examinations conducted in workplaces and on changes of residence.[49]

• • •

The continuing militarized division of the country, and the endless confrontation with the United States, the globe's major (and now only) superpower, helped shape North Korea's exceptional degree of social, military, and political cohesion around highly concentrated leadership in the Korean Workers Party and the armed forces and continues to help legitimize and sustain the monolithic *Juche* regime. As in the guerrilla bands of the 1930s, discipline, leadership, and loyalty came to be represented as crucial values as long as the country remained under siege. Until the siege is lifted, the abnormal situation is likely to continue. A more normal internal political practice can only be hoped for (which does not mean that it would necessarily follow quickly or smoothly) after the achievement of some degree of normalcy in North Korea's relations with the United States, Japan, and above all South Korea. Today, however, demands by neighboring states and especially the Bush administration that North Korea "normalize" itself first are seen but as a new form of siege, compelling the partisan state to regroup and resist.

The regime is caught in a dilemma: While Kim Jong Il and some of those surrounding him may realize the need to open the country to new technology, capital, ideas, and trade, they are fearful that such an opening might bring with it "degenerate capitalist phenomena" such as "thieves, punks or pimps,"[50] and thereby jeopardize the carefully constructed system of control and the prospects for long dynastic rule. The role of the leaders would diminish to the extent the country was opened and North Koreans began to be able to penetrate the web of sycophancy, deceit, bombast, and irrationality that has been spun around them and to fulfill their *Juche*-promised destiny as "masters of creation."

As the "family state" of imperial Japan was reproduced in the family state of North Korea, the cult of the Kims came to resemble the cult that surrounded Kim Il Sung's old enemy, the emperor. Fascist Japan and contemporary North Korea shared a rejection of Western individualism and rationalism and an insistence on the superiority of the national collective under the supposedly benign rule of an ultimate leader. Where the imperial family was "the fountain source of the Japanese nation" and the great duty of the Japanese people was "to guard and maintain the Imperial Throne," in North Korea the family of the Leader became the embodiment and moral essence of the race and the people were called upon to unite around him in terms that echo those of the Japanese texts of the 1930s. By the 1970s, leader worship and *Juche* had mutated into a parody of the Japanese imperial state.

The philosophical and cultural, as distinct from the military and political, problem that North Korea faces is the same one that has been faced by all of former Confucian east Asia: how to substitute a sense of individual moral autonomy, or citizenship, for the notions of collective identity rooted in tradition. In Japan, the prewar collective identity of *kokutai* (national polity) was only slowly transformed in this direction after 1945, and many still hanker for a return to the warmth and security of the national collective. The debates about "subjectivity" that raged there in the early postwar decades will no doubt be repeated in some future North Korea. In China, communist ideologues struggled to soften communist rule by constructing a family state under Mao as the grand patriarch, but the country's vastness and diversity defied representation as a single family and in recent decades the market seems to have substituted for all ideologies. In South Korea, the generation born in the 1960s and educated in the 1980s fought against military and fascist representations of collective nationhood, but the process of constituting selfhood and citizenship as the core of political culture remains far from complete. North Korea's cultural crisis therefore has much in common with its neighbor states.

Pyongyang's spokespersons now seek nothing so much as

the assurance that, whatever happens, its political system will be preserved—that is, its leader will not be deposed, which was very much the central worry in 1945 of the defeated Japanese, who repeatedly insisted on assurances that the emperor system would continue. If the analogy holds, retention of the North Korean leader might be the condition for allowing sweeping social and cultural change in North Korea, as retention of the emperor allowed Japan to bridge the transition from the defeat and collapse of the old order to construction of a new one.

Amid reports of spreading corruption, bribery, pilfering, absenteeism, and noncompliance, North Korea's repressive system may well be loosening. As systems of production and reproduction break down, the control system too comes under heavy pressure. People can no longer be provided with food and shelter, and the party has all but vanished. The basis of faith, the *Juche* ideology, looks to many of its practitioners increasingly hollow. The flow of defectors grows, and increasingly they are from the "reliable," elite echelons of the regime—soldiers, border police, security officials, school-teachers, hospital administrators, professors, weapons scientists.[51] Refugees speak in vengeful terms of overthrowing the regime in order to achieve liberation, because, as one refugee put it, "It would be better if war broke out and everything would be smashed so that a great change can take place."[52]

The faith of the people is stretched to the limit. When Kim Jong Il contemplates the combination of catastrophic natural conditions that have struck the country since he assumed its helm and the international encirclement that slowly tightens around him, he must wonder whether the heavens might have turned against him. He must know that in the Confucian tradition the loss of heaven's mandate to rule is signified by natural calamities and inexplicable phenomena and that the sanction that follows is transfer of the mandate to a more worthy claimant, the process that modern times came to call revolution. Throughout east Asia, however absolute the sovereignty of a monarch or ruler, ultimate sovereignty in the moral sense rested in the hands of the people.

North Korea's *Juche* world may be the most coherent, politically engineered system in history, but it already has a phantasmagoric character. However brilliantly imagined, created, and sustained by its artist and scenario-writer, the theater magic depends in the long run on a mass suspension of disbelief. Ever harder it is to sustain, the plainer it becomes that the *Juche* world can no longer feed, clothe, and educate its citizens and the more that other and better worlds come to be glimpsed through the cracks in the theater walls. The *Juche* world begins to look as if it had been designed by some Korean Disney as a "*Juche* World."

# THE <u>JUCHE</u> WORLD: GROWTH TO COLLAPSE

North Korea, the more industrialized region of the peninsula prior to the Korean War, surpassed the southern Republic of Korea in growth during the 1950s and 1960s before entering a slow decline as its plant rotted or became obsolescent and resources were drained into the military or used to shore up the cult of the leader and his family, and in the 1990s the country was buffeted by a series of natural disasters—flood, drought, famine—even as the confrontation with the United States steadily sharpened.

The truth of the North Korean economic record has also become clearer in recent years, and, as in other areas, the more that is known the blacker the outlook. Assessment is complicated by the fact that the government publishes only select statistics, those invariably designed to impress rather than inform, and North Korean sources rarely refer to foreign aid, which particularly in the country's early decades was very substantial. In the 1940s and 1950s, "fraternal" socialist aid was sent from the Eastern bloc, and in the 1990s and beyond grain arrived from international organizations, capitalist countries, and NGOs. North Korea is a planned, socialist economy, and, for the plan to have any chance of functioning a reliable, scientific structure of information gathering must be developed and arbitrary interventions minimized. In this sense, unsurprisingly, the "cult" and the "plan" are at odds, and it has been increasingly difficult to protect the latter from the frenzied excesses and arbitrary interventions of the former. There must be doubt, as a result, as to whether even the regime itself has access to real economic data.

Kim Il Sung promised as early as 1962 that once the 1963 production targets were met, the working people of the country would be able to "lead a rich life, living in tile-roofed houses, having rice and meat, and wearing fine clothes." In 1970 he claimed that the food problem "has been solved completely." Similar claims have been made from time to time ever since. The 1992 New Year editorial of the *Pyongyang Times* proclaimed it still a "long-cherished desire" of the people and a "major goal . . . in socialist construction" that people should be able to "dine regularly on polished rice and broth, wear silk clothes and live in a house with a tiled roof." For many, however, that modest goal has receded steadily into dreamland.

Today, daily life for most people is lived in the cold and dark, and about half of the school-age population no longer attends school, instead wandering the streets while their parents forage for food. The population of homeless drifters grows.[1] Satellite night photographs show North Korea as an eerily dark spot on the earth's surface. Nothing is more plain than that North Korea, after half a century, has failed its people.

In the early decades, land reform, planning, aid from the socialist bloc, and concentrated effort produced promising results. Cambridge economist Joan Robinson, visiting it in 1964, wrote of "patriotic rage and devotion expressing itself in enthusiasm for hard work." Her overall assessment was that "all the economic miracles of the postwar world are put in the shade by these achievements."[2] A decade later, the prospects still seemed bright. The "self-reliant" North Korean economic model appeared "well on the way towards the economic structure of an advanced industrial state," with the expectation of becoming "a small industrial country on the model of Austria, East Germany, Sweden and Switzerland."[3] Another scholar commented, "[T]he achievements of the Korean Workers Party are clearly remarkable and will be remembered long after the tottering neo-colony in South Korea has finally collapsed."[4] In retrospect, such judgments were plainly mistaken, but they seemed plausible at the time (and this author then helped publish them). Certainly, the evidence was at best ambiguous. As late as 1976, even the CIA thought North Korea was surpassing South Korea in almost every sector of the economy.[5] The cooking of the books was not then obvious, and the strains, excesses, and distortions as the regime's priorities shifted from growth to ensuring the succession of Kim Jong Il were only beginning to be felt economically.

The regime claimed that, despite the harshness of the North's climate and the difficulty of the terrain—less than 20 percent of which was suitable for agriculture—output rose by an annual average of 10 percent during the 1950s and 6.3 percent during the 1960s. In the 1970s the country began exporting rice—not so much an indication of a surplus as of the desire to earn foreign exchange, while importing cheaper grains for domestic consumption. Enormous efforts were devoted to civil engineering projects designed to increase crop acreage by reclamation or the clearing of forest lands and to raising agricultural (and fishery) productivity. By 1979, North Korea was claiming world-record figures for rice yield per hectare. The United Nations Food and Agriculture Organization (FAO) accepted that North Korea was indeed number one in this from 1979 to 1990, which put it ahead of other major rice producers such as Japan and South Korea or smaller, but very efficient, ones like Australia. It was held to be more than three times as efficient as Thailand and significantly better than the United States.[6] In terms of calorie intake, too, North Korea claimed to be performing better for its people than South Korea throughout the 1980s. Not until 1991 did FAO revise its figures, giving a (marginal) statistical superiority to South Korea.[7] Soon afterward, the North plunged into the direst of famines, and such statistics were discarded as useless.

From 1990, conditions steadily worsened, shortages grew even more severe, and food riots were occasionally reported. Not only was food rationed, and rice reduced to 30 to 40 percent of other, coarser grains such as millet (far less outside Pyongyang), but food was increasingly available only on the black market. Meat, if available at all, was restricted to national holidays. Then the country entered upon its blackest period, the catastrophic famine years of 1994–97. Severe flooding occurred in successive years, followed in 1997 by a drought. Harvests fell steadily. With a minimum requirement of approximately five million tons of grain per year to feed its population even at minimal levels, according to the UN World Food Program, production fell to around 2.36 million tons in 1996 and 2.66 million tons in 1997.[8] The combination of flood, drought, and loss of electric power and fuel would have been devastating even if the North Koreans hadn't been living in the delusional *Juche* world. Fields that had produced six tons per hectare in 1987 were raising one-twentieth of that by 1996. Where the state had been providing 700 kilograms of grain per year for a family of three, that was slashed to 270 kilograms, enough for two bowls of rice per person per day.[9] By 2002, even that had been stopped.

Despite the launch of a large-scale international relief effort, especially targeting children, there were many deaths, especially among the most vulnerable members of the population. Nobody knows how many famine victims there were, but estimates range from 220,000, a figure calculated from government statements on birth and death rates, to three million, the latter a worst-case and almost certainly exaggerated scenario.[10] Malnutrition and stunting of growth among children became chronic and, years after the worst had passed, 40 percent of children under five are still seriously malnourished.[11] As of 2003, although the harvest shortfall was still estimated at about one million tons,[12] the UN was having great difficulty persuading donor countries to fill in the gap.

Not only were the claims of *Juche* food miracles and the world's best productivity abandoned, but the modest-sounding goals set out by Kim Il Sung in 1962 came to seem not just unattainable but fantastic. In the early nineties, people were encouraged to confine themselves to two meals a day; by the midnineties they were lucky if they could manage that. In the early years of the twenty-first century a desperate effort is being made to promote potato cultivation, and people are being taught to make potato cakes, potato pancakes, and so on. Kim Jong Il is said to have declared, "It is the same as rice and henceforth we will have it as staple and not as subsidiary."[13] The sequence of appalling natural catastrophes that followed upon the death of the Great Leader in 1994 might have suggested to some that the regime's "mandate from heaven" was running out. Like the other "natural" disasters of the twentieth century, these plainly had both natural and human causes.

A certain kind of high growth may have been briefly attained, especially in 1950s and 1960s, from *Juche* agriculture, but it is hard now to distinguish statistical fact from political braggadocio, and the achievements, such as they were, brought a high cost because the agricultural development model was unsustainable from the start. Filled with Promethean confidence, it showed little respect for or understanding of nature, instead insisting that "man is master of nature . . . and decides everything." Exploitation was maximized; mountains and hillsides cleared and cultivated; large swathes of coastal wetland were reclaimed.[14] Targets, once set, had to be met in order to satisfy the vanity of the Leader and his counsels, irrespective of the consequences. The floods and drought that swept the country in the mid-1990s were a devastating demonstration of the failure of the command economy as a management system on the one hand, and of the failure of communist belief in the ability to utterly manipulate and control nature on the other.[15]

The best estimates are that industrial output might have grown at an average of about 6.3 percent between 1985 and 1990, although crucial sectors like electric power lagged and wastage levels were high. However, the growth rate for the economy seems to have dropped from around two percent in 1989 to minus 3.7 percent in 1990 and minus 5.2 percent in 1991, making those the worst years since the Korean War ended. By 1990, per capita GNP in the North ($1,038) was already only about one-sixth of the South's ($6,498).[16] There had been virtually no growth at all for a full decade. But that was merely the beginning of decline. By the end of the nineties the South-North differential was between 8:1 and 11:1 and steadily widening.[17] The official target for the third Seven-Year Plan (1987–93) had been for an average annual growth rate of 10 percent, but between 1993 and 1996 the economy declined by about 50 percent and per capita income dropped to $481, according to joint research by the United Nations Development Program and the North Korean government; plan targets were shelved.[18]

Electric power generation during the 1990s declined by 60–70 percent—to levels so low that the entire country was running on the same amount of power as a medium-sized American city.[19] Coal and fertilizer production dropped by more than 50 percent, factory productivity by around 70 percent.[20] Things improved little in the new century. South Korean bank estimates were for a modest growth in the

Northern economy in 2001, but the CIA calculated a further contraction of about 3 percent. Power generation is now estimated at about 15 percent of that of the South, and more than half of that is lost in transmission, via underground cables that have long been degenerating and are extremely difficult to repair. By 2002, factories had been idling for more than a decade, producing at only a fraction of their capacity due to the breakdown of the system of supply and transportation of materials, the collapse of the electric power supply, and the decline of industrial plant. Imports of oil were slashed, transport and communications broke down, large-scale army maneuvers ceased, while air force pilots were reduced to a few hours practice per year (takeoffs and landings, but no combat flights).

The planners in Pyongyang were neither blind to, nor ignorant of the problems that plagued them. From the mid-1970s, while maintaining the rhetoric of *Juche* autarchy and self-reliance, they made considerable efforts to reengage with the global, capitalist economy. Three decades of such efforts, however, have produced little in the way of discernible results.

Following the "oil shock" of 1973 when the economy was first opened to trade with and the import of plant from European and other capitalist countries, energy prices rose and export prices, especially for North Korea's nonferrous minerals, plummeted. Unable to pay its debts, North Korea defaulted. In fact it has defaulted several times, and each default has soured its relations further with the capitalist world. To compensate, and to try to adhere to the ambitious growth targets of the plans, exploitation of the workforce was stepped up. Mass campaigns, thought by many to reflect the hand of Kim Jong Il, then attempting to make his mark, were launched. The anti-Japan partisans of the 1930s, his father's heroic band, were adopted as the model for emulation in all areas of life. These were years of maximum Cultural Revolution disturbance in China, and that influence was also plain in the "three revolutions" teams that were dispatched to workplaces across North Korea, charged to achieve productivity gains by a revolution in ideology, technology, and culture. "Struggle campaigns" were launched, first for seventy days, later for 200, even 2,000 days,[21] but the reliance on frenzied, Stakhanovite-style productivity campaigns (the "speed of the eighties") brought ever diminishing returns. People grew tired; machines began to wear out; and top-down planning methods failed to develop mechanisms of flexibility and consumer feedback.

The much-trumpeted "self-reliance" of the North Korean development model also concealed a high degree of reliance on Soviet aid. Most major industrial installations were built with Soviet technical assistance and financed by Soviet credit (little of which was ever repaid). From 1991, as "commercial" terms replaced "friendship" terms in trade with both Russia and China, imports of fuel sank and industry as well as agriculture fell into deep, structural crisis. In addition, the constant drain of scarce resources into military-related industries, including missile research and production, over such a long period enfeebled the nonmilitary sector and reduced its capacity to meet basic social needs, even though it might have produced some positive economic effect. A burgeoning weapons export sector accounted for up to one third of exports in the 1980s, about $4 billion worth between 1981 and 1988, though this income was appropriated exclusively by the military for its own purposes. The precise measure of the economy directly controlled by the military is uncertain, but estimates range between 20 and 50 percent, and the shadow of defense priority hangs over everything. The cost of building much of the industrial and military infrastructure in underground structures, and of constructing the Pyongyang subway system at depths of up to 100 meters, was prodigious. Perhaps most important, the megalomania of the leadership cult imposed serious strains on the economy.

As his family was equated with the state, all forms of culture and economy were required to speak its glory. The development of Pyongyang as a monument to the Kim family soaked up money that might have been used elsewhere.

Construction commenced in 1984 on the 105-story, 3,000-room Ryugyong Hotel, scheduled for completion in readiness for the thirteenth World Festival of Youth and Students of 1989. Concrete facade crumbling, it remains uncompleted to this day. The ghostly edifice has developed a Pisa-ish tilt that defies engineers, and its elevator system and toilets have yet to be installed. Huge resources were also lavished on facilities to host other major events in Pyongyang. Hundreds of millions, if not billions, of dollars were spent on the various facilities for these 1989 games, which were meant to rival the Seoul Olympics of the previous year. Inevitably, Pyongyang's event was upstaged by Seoul's. Little world attention was accorded to the Pyongyang events save for astonishment at the lavish "mass games, " in which 50,000 people were mobilized in giant pantomines designed to spell out revolutionary scenes or messages of loyalty and love for the Great Leader.

This was outdone in April 1992 at the eightieth birthday celebration for the Great Leader, which cost an estimated $1 billion and involved 100,000 people in mass games. In 2002, at the Arirang Games, mass gymnastic and artistic performances were on a similar scale.

In short, North Korea, and especially its capital, was turned into a land of monuments, filled with the temples and shrines of state orthodoxy. As in the ancient Egypt of the pharaohs, the primary call on all resources was for the glorification of the leader. A substantial industry was also devoted exclusively to the production and promotion of hagiography devoted to the great and dear leaders in all the main languages of the world. The entire nation was caught up in the throes of this mass quasi-religious movement.

The glorification of the Kim family became the principle to which all else, including economic sense, was subordinate. The price, however, was that economic plans had to be scrapped. The primary call on public resources became the sustenance and promotion of the the Kim family. Its apparently insatiable craving for recognition and deference gradually drained and exhausted both state and society.

*Juche* as a model of international development was promoted and for a time exercised a considerable attraction in parts of the communist world and Third World. Teams of North Korean engineers and technicians were dispatched to Africa, around 5,000 at its peak in the 1980s, in an effort to establish the North Korean model as the key to development there. Full embassies were opened throughout Africa, at a time when even Britain was cutting back on its diplomatic presence on the continent for cost reasons.[22] North Korea was involved in military training in some cases, or simply in economic development on "friendly" terms.

Kim Il Sung seems to have responded to flattery and been attracted by the idea of having grand stadiums named after him somewhere in Africa.[23] In May 1978, "Emperor" Bokassa of Central Africa was feted in Pyongyang, where Kim Il Sung announced that the two countries enjoyed "an identity of the aspirations for the building of an independent new society." Bokassa's reign as self-proclaimed emperor was blessedly short. Subsequently sentenced to death for war crimes, including cannibalism, he is commonly regarded today as one of twentieth-century Africa's most bloodthirsty monsters. Apart from Bokassa, the techniques of the Kim cult were studied, and relations were close with many of the world's most brutal and infamous regimes, including those of Mobutu in Zaire, Macias Nguema in Equatorial Guinea, Idi Amin in Uganda, Pol Pot in Cambodia, Gaddafi in Libya, and Ceausescu in Romania. Didier Ratsiraka, who was Madagascar's president for twenty-three years, was a regular visitor to Pyongyang for Kim Il Sung's birthday. His attitude apparently so pleased the Great Leader that he ordered the construction in marble of a splendid palace for his friend.[24] Ratsiraka appears to have tried to adapt *Juche* socialism in his country, which sank ever deeper into poverty. Eventually he fled into exile with his family and retinue.[25] Somali admirers could expect invitations, including on occasions a chartered plane, to bring them to study the secrets of *Juche* agriculture.[26] Romania's Ceausescu was a particularly close ally right up until his regime collapsed ignominiously and he was executed in December 1989.

All of this was not only disastrous in terms of the friends, allies, and causes that North Korea chose to support, but because it drew resources away from North Korea's own development. Whether the aid rendered to Africa left any lasting benefit is hard to know. Certainly by the end of the century the idea that North Korea might, in any way, be seen as a model of development was laughable.

## SEARCHING FOR REFORM FORMULAS

The myth of economic autarchy, sustained by the myth of guerrilla survival against all odds, has died hard in North Korea, if died it has. Kim Jong Il continues to stress emulation of the army's "undying and absolute sacrificing spirit" as the way to solve economic problems.[27] Yet, at the same time, between 1996 and 2002, relations were normalized with many countries, including most of western Europe (with the exception of France), Australia, Malaysia, Brazil, Turkey, Cambodia, Kuwait, and Russia. Kim also made a series of overseas visits, including China and Russia in 2001, where he inspected production facilities and contemplated practices that might usefully be adopted in North Korea. Teams of bureaucrats, politicians, and experts were dispatched to scour the world for development models and technical and financial assistance. Nearly five hundred students were sent off in 2001 alone to countries such as China, Australia, Italy, and Sweden.[28] A great many seemed to be bent on learning Western market economics.

In the eighties, Pyongyang had sought to breathe new life into the economy by encouraging joint ventures with other countries, including capitalist ones. However, the unresolved debt problem and the general insecurity surrounding the future of the country meant that major Western or multinational corporations were not attracted, and it was almost exclusively Koreans in Japan who set up shop, mostly in textiles and food processing. Their experience was an unhappy one of bureaucratic intervention, incompetence, and confusion. By 1993, only twenty of the original 120 joint ventures were left.[29]

In 1991, a different approach was tried. The regime announced the establishment of the Rajin-Sonbong Special Zone located close to North Korea's frontier with Russia and China at the mouth of the Tumen River. A vast expanse of frontier land—742 square kilometers—its target was to draw in $47 billion in

**The Four Special Economic Zones**
map courtesy of Pyongyong Square

direct foreign investment by 2010 and to become a kind of "northern Shenzhen" (the booming Chinese "special zone" adjacent to Hong Kong). However, despite being adopted as a UN project in 1994, its remote location and a heavy Pyongyang hand on the tiller proved significant disincentives. By the end of 2000, only around $600 million had been invested there.[30] Although it was hoped that the zone would turn into a heavy and chemical industry center, its most successful venture to date has been a casino opened in 2000 by the Hong Kong–based Emperor group. It functions on a twenty-four-hour-a-day basis, drawing in mainly Chinese and Russian customers, and has developed a reputation as an exotic gambling mecca.

In 1998, a further special zone aimed at attracting foreign capital from tourism was opened at Mt. Kumgang, as a joint development with South Korea's huge conglomerate, Hyundai, in a mountain district with sacred significance to all Koreans. Hyundai also agreed to pay a lump sum of $942 million by 2005 plus $12 million monthly for the monopoly rights to the tourism ventures.[31] Tours there started in 1998. In the first four years, half a million South Koreans have made the trip via a boat that carried almost 1,400 passengers, almost as a pilgrimage, and substantial revenues were funneled to Pyongyang. At $300 per passenger, if all berths on the boat were filled it would earn Pyongyang $450 million a year in licensing fees.[32] The South Korean visitors were carefully quarantined from any contact with ordinary North Koreans. They even traveled by segregated routes from the North Korean harbor, but conflicts still sometimes arose with their North Korean guides. In February 2003, a first group of 500 politicians, scholars, and businesspeople crossed the Demilitarized Zone by bus, opening a much easier and faster route. The Mt. Kumgang area was declared a "Special Tourism Zone" and Hyundai is still considering developing major tourism facilities there, including ski lifts, hotels, golf courses, pubs and bars, and a "silver town" with special facilities to attract the elderly. In October, a convoy of buses conveyed north the largest Southern contingent in half a century: 1,100 people setting off to attend the opening of a gymnasium in Pyongyang, to play a basketball game there, and to hand over a gift of 1,000 head of cattle.

Hyundai's enthusiasm for the project seems to have exceeded the bounds of commercial sense. Any such business is risky. Negotiations with Northern officials are said to have been frustrating and hard, and profit may not accrue, if at all, until some point in the indefinite future. In the lead-up to the Pyongyang summit of 2000, Hyundai was involved in the transfer of a still-to-be-accounted-for sum of $500 million to Kim's regime, a matter that was three years later the subject of arrests and investigations in the south. Hyundai also found itself in a serious financial crisis, at least partly because of its commitment to North Korea, and in 2002 the South Korean government had to come to the rescue of the Mt. Kumgang tourism venture.

In September of that year, a special law was passed to set up a Sinuiju Special Economic Zone on the North Korean side of the Yalu River frontier, opposite the Chinese city of Dandong. The existing population of the region, some half million people, was slated to be moved out to accommodate an influx of young, skilled Chinese and Korean workers, in a walled, capitalist enclave of international finance, trade, commerce, industry, advanced technology, leisure, and tourism. Its currency was to be the U.S. dollar, and it would be administered independently, with its own passports and flag, its own legislature, judiciary, and administration, with no border duties and no capital controls.

The plan, however, began inauspiciously when the newly appointed governor, a millionaire Chinese businessman (with Dutch citizenship), was detained by authorities in China over alleged tax and other financial irregularities. In July 2003 Chinese courts gave him an eighteen-year sentence and fined him approximately $9 million.[33] It was clearly a less-than-diplomatic signal from the Chinese about the prospect of a potential haven for hot money, speculators, gamblers, and others likely to be drawn to such an unregulated environment just over the border from China. In April 2003, however, South Korean sources said that direction of the project had passed to Chang Sung Taek, Kim Jong Il's brother-in-law, and that he had been conducting meetings with potential investors from Canada, Hong Kong, Australia, and Taiwan.[34] The project, not unlike earlier grandiose international projects, remains in limbo.

At South-North working-level talks in Pyongyang in November 2002 a Southern proposal coming from the Hyundai Asan Corporation and the state-run Korean Land Corporation for yet another Special Economic Zone at Kaesong, less than 70 kilometers north of Seoul and about 160 kilometers south of Pyongyang, was formally adopted.

Such a regional development would be different in several key respects from the other special zones. Situated on the about-to-be-reopened rail line between the two capitals, it would have easy access to Seoul's newly developed Incheon International Airport and—if plans went ahead as hoped—it would be on a grand scale: comprising ultimately a twenty-eight-square-kilometer (6,900-acre) industrial park, attracting $2 billion in investment, first in light industry (footwear, textiles, electric, and electronic assembly) and later in petrochemical products, auto parts, semiconductors, and the like. Twenty-thousand people would be employed in 150 enterprises within the first year, those figures rising to 80,000 workers and 600 enterprises within five to eight years.[35] The major attraction for investors is the prospect of a skilled and disciplined workforce, with each worker available at $65 a month (while a similar worker in South Korea would earn $2,000). In addition, for South Korean investors, there would be neither language nor cultural barriers.[36] The commitment of the South Korean government and some major corporations, and the closeness to major population centers, trade routes, and markets, made this project more feasible than either of its antecedents. It takes only an hour to go from Hyundai's head office in Seoul to Kaesong, about as much time as could easily be spent in a Seoul traffic jam without getting anywhere.[37]

The Kaesong project is inevitably tied to the projected reopening of the connecting railway, a project agreed to at the South-North summit talks in 2000, which has implications not only for economic exchanges but also as a harbinger and symbol of national unity. In June 2003, the land mines laid by both sides in the Demilitarized Zone had been cleared from the trackway and a ceremony to commemorate the completion of most of the work was held. The Unification Ministry in Seoul announced that it expected trains to be running by September (later revised to December). Pyongyang could expect a significant "rental" income from the opening of the through-freight route across North Korea to China, Russia, and Europe.[38]

The record, it has to be said, is not good so far in any of the "Special Economic Zones," but the strength of commitment may have grown over the years and the insistence on isolating the capitalist "virus" from the *Juche* world may have weakened as well. It was noticeable at least that each of the experimental economic zones moved steadily closer to population centers and to Pyongyang.

In July 2002, paralleling these steps toward the creation of special economic zones, a series of drastic economic reforms were adopted, affecting virtually all aspects of economic life. The rationing of goods was suddenly abolished for all but a very few categories of consumer products. Where the state had long distributed through its rationing system all sorts of basic goods, including soap, toothpaste, tobacco, matches, clothing, shoes, food, bean paste, and salt, all controls were suspended in practice during the 1990s and formally from 2002. State subsidies for education, childcare, welfare, and education also ceased. People would pay "market" rates for such services in future. Wages were increased by large amounts and differentiated by category in terms of social productivity, with important categories of workers such as coal miners given twenty-fold increases. An ordinary worker on a monthly salary of 110 *won* might suddenly find herself receiving 1,000 *won*, and a coal miner 6,000 *won*.[39] Salary increases ranged from a minimum of nine- to twelvefold for doctors, eighteen- to twenty-fold for coal miners, and twenty-five- to thirty-one-fold for army officers.[40] Services hitherto provided free, however, were henceforth subject to charge, with public transportation fees alone twenty times higher. The purchase price paid to farmers for rice rose by more than 500 times while the price paid by consumers rose by a similar proportion, from 0.08 *won* per kilo to 43 *won* per kilo, steadily rising thereafter as inflation set in and reportedly hitting 250 *won* per kilo in April 2003.[41] Food alone came to consume two-thirds of the newly inflated salaries. The won, the national currency, was devalued in 2002 to one-seventieth of its existing value (from approximately 2.5 to 150 *won* to the dollar), and then again slashed to 900 won to the dollar in the summer of 2003. Early in 2003, a national network of black markets, which had grown out of the need to cope with the breakdown of the supply system, especially of food, was officially recognized and transformed to legal status.

These were dramatic developments. A senior North Korean government official declared, "We are reforming the economic system on the basis of profitability"—using for the first time in fifty years the word *kaehyok*, (reform), and thus conceding that the system had been less than perfect.[42] The *Asian Wall St. Journal* was on the mark in its assessment: "With the DPRK economy in a shambles and the state system of production and rationing in disarray, the government has had no choice but to let the people fend for themselves in the open market."[43] Whatever the motive, such a step is likely to prove irrevocable. By scrapping centralized economic controls in favor of market principles for the determining of wages and prices, Pyongyang was opening the door to capitalism.

It appeared to be moving with a kind of desperate haste. The grandeur of Hyundai's plans for North Korea contrasted sharply with the reality of continuing economic crisis, the virtual collapse of the energy sector, the near collapse of manufacturing and mining, and drastic cuts in agricultural production due to shockingly bad natural conditions and a decline in chemical fertilizer production. From the mid-1990s, North Korea became best known to the world for its famine and for its steady flow of refugees, especially into neighboring China.

The special zones were an attempt to open beneficial economic relations with the capitalist world and to secure direct foreign investment to renew the country's decrepit infrastructure. However, North Korean officials have been badly hobbled by fears of possible "spiritual pollution" that might subvert the monolith-like "purity" of the guerrilla state. It is an impossible dilemma, as China discovered some twenty years ago: Capitalism and "spiritual pollution" go hand in hand.

The lack of capital or export commodities suitable for world markets has led Pyongyang to adopt some highly unorthodox policies. Starting sometime in the 1970s, it had recourse to narcotics, counterfeiting, smuggling, and arms (including missile) sales, and that commitment has strengthened with time. Missile sales are estimated by U.S. military sources to amount to around $580 million per year as of 2001, but probably were reduced sharply thereafter because of tightened international controls.[44] As for the narcotics, counterfeiting, and smuggling operations, in entering these fields *as a matter of state policy*, North Korea may well be unique. While the full details of the decision-making are unclear, one plausible account has it that Kim Il Sung in 1992 personally ordered the country's frontier regions to set themselves up in appropriate businesses, including opium cultivation, and to seek fiscal autonomy from the national government.[45] In this, too, he would have been aping the Japanese, whose Kwantung Army sought fiscal autonomy by opium cultivation in these same areas in the 1930s and 1940s.

Hwang Jang-yop, the former top Pyongyang official who defected in 1997, refers to opium as "the new North Korean cash crop," its cultivation and preparation conducted under the auspices of the army, the National Security Bureau, and the police.[46] He mentions a directive issued by the State Council (the country's highest state organ, functioning akin to a cabinet) in June 1994 calling for the "introduction of good seeds and proper cultivation methods from Southeast Asia, as well as establishing trade routes." By 1999, the U.S. State Department was reporting that a stretch of between 4,500 and 7,000 hectares of poppy fields were under cultivation near the border with China, producing between thirty and forty-five tons of opium per year. When the floods of 1996 wiped out a lot of these fields, much effort went to develop the production and distribution of amphetamines, with the Japanese market especially in mind.[47]

During the nineties North Koreans, mostly diplomats, were arrested or expelled on narcotic charges from Sweden, Finland, Estonia, Russia, Germany, Egypt, China, Nepal, Cameroon, Guinea, Kenya, Zambia, Thailand, and Cambodia.[48] In April 1997, Japanese customs authorities confiscated a shipment of sixty-five kilos of stimulants from a North Korean ship,[49] and in April 2003, a fifty-kilogram consignment of pure heroin was found on a North Korean owned and crewed ship, the *Pong Su*, off the coast of Australia.[50] Japanese authorities estimate that about 80 percent of the amphetamines and 40 percent of the other drugs entering Japan originate in North Korea.[51] Authorities in Seoul estimate that North Korea is producing about forty tons of opium annually, making it the world's third-largest producer.[52] Earnings from heroin, cocaine, and methamphetamine are estimated at approximately $100 million per year. The process of growing, cultivating, and refining such drugs could not be undertaken without endorsement from the top. Japanese and Russian crime syndicates are thought to be Pyongyang's overseas partners.

In mid-2003, it was this issue on which Washington was focusing attention. Some protested that the opium and heroin charges were part of a Washington-centered "psy-war" campaign against Pyongyang, in part because Kim Jong Il has said that he abhors drugs and has ordered both dealers and addicts to be shot and "Chinese merchants" dealing in drugs to be caned and sent back to China.[53] One—unlikely—explanation is that "rogue elements within the penumbras of the increasingly amorphous DPRK government, especially its foreign trade establishment posted overseas, some local military commanders and special services apparatus" might be responsible.[54] Whatever the explanation, North Korea's proven drug connections might make it easier for the Bush administration to organize a coalition to cooperate in putting pressure on it since, as the veteran American diplomat and author Kenneth Quinones remarks, all states opposed drug trading.[55] Protestations of innocence will do little to dent the spreading international conviction of Kim Jong Il's guilt so long as the trade continues.

Counterfeiting operations, especially targeting the U.S. $100 bill, have been widely reported since the mid-1990s.[56] However, although North Korea seems to be able to produce high quality notes, it lacks the equipment to test and discriminate between real and fake; both now circulate in North Korea itself. Relatively petty smuggling operations have also often been reported since the 1970s, sometimes just involving the use of diplomatic privilege to smuggle whisky or delicacies to the Dear Leader's table. A senior North Korean diplomat who defected in 1991 reported that one task of the country's diplomatic missions was "to procure for Kim Jong Il supplies of Hennessy cognac in France, crabs in Norway, Black Sea caviar and even the livers of blue sharks fished off the Angolan coast."[57]

Three years into the new century, North Korea resembled nothing so much as Japan in the last stages of the Pacific and China wars in 1945—chronic shortages of food, factories not working, transport and communications in chaos, people reduced to selling anything they possess in order to get food, and a psychological mood of exhaustion and tension in anticipation of some final cataclysm.[58] Pyongyang seems to have decided that it will be impossible to achieve its goals unless relations with Japan and the United States are normalized. While that may be true, it is also true that the modern, industrial transformation of the country is blocked by its feudal and dynastic politics. Real economic change depends on real political change. The problem is how to find a lever to address simultaneously these two blockages.

# THE KOREAS: ONE PLUS ONE EQUALS ONE

Sharing with North Korea a culture, a language, and a peninsula, South Korea naturally has a distinctive perspective on the *Juche* world and its ruler. When George Bush issued his "axis of evil" statement in Seoul, it was typically seen by a former foreign service officer there as "diplomatically wayward, strategically unwise, and historically immoral."[1] When Tokyo vents paroxysms of rage at Pyongyang over its handling of its abducted citizens or Washington denounces the North over the latest nuclear revelation, Seoul's response is invariably measured. Both Kim Dae Jung, president of the republic of Korea from 1998 to 2003, and his successor, Roh Moo-Hyun, have insisted that force or even international sanctions are out of the question and dialogue is the only way to resolve all problems on the peninsula. As tension escalated between Pyongyang and Washington in the fall of 2002, exchanges between Seoul and Pyongyang continued unabated. A top-level delegation from the North, including the chair of North Korea's State Planning Committee and Kim Jong Il's brother-in-law, a powerful figure in the Korean Workers' Party, flew in to Seoul on October 26 for a nine-day tour of semiconductor, car, chemical, and steel plants,[2] while, despite disparaging signals from Washington, work continued toward reconnecting the railway link between Korea's two severed parts for the first time since 1950.

With a Gross Domestic Product now thirteen times that of the North and double its population,[3] South Korea's confidence stems from political and economic maturity. After almost four decades of military rule, the South's democratic revolution in 1987 consolidated the autonomy of civil society, deepening confidence and further reducing fear of the North. Its political democracy, prosperity, and advanced industrial society contrast ever more starkly with North Korea's poverty, totalitarianism, and desperation.

Colonialism, occupation, war, and the entrenched partition systems have left the peninsula as a whole painfully scarred, and the "normal" national aspirations of its people—the ancient kingdom of Korea unified since AD 668—frustrated. Ironically, though divided and in confrontation now for fifty years, both Koreas were saddled with states that were strong vertically (against their own populations) but weak horizontally (against outside pressures from other powers).[4] Before, during, and after the Korean War, the Republic of Korea was governed by repressive and brutal dictatorial regimes. Kidnapping, torture, and a many-faceted denial of human rights were justified by the anticommunist imperative of the Cold War and given *carte blanche* by the firm backing of the United States. Between 1967 and 1969, over one hundred students, artists, and intellectuals who were studying or resident in Europe and North America were essentially kidnapped, dragged back to Seoul, and accused of spying for North Korea. They were tortured, tried, and a number of them sentenced to death or long terms of imprisonment. A few years later, in 1973, Kim Dae Jung (later to be president) was abducted by agents of the South Korean CIA from a Tokyo hotel room. He barely escaped with his life, and the affair was quietly buried by the two governments. The state terror of the South Korean military regime—backed by the United States and Japan—reached its apogee in the Kwangju massacre of 1980, when hundreds of students and citizens protesting the imposition of martial law as the regime cracked down on the democratic opposition were slaughtered. Only the triumph of a popular citizens' movement put an end to it.

From South Korea's capital, Seoul, it is but thirty miles up the road to the DMZ, and another 120 to Pyongyang. Spies, special agents, and on occasion assassins have crossed and re-crossed this line, engaging in various missions from which thousands did not return. Officially, since the end of the Korean War, there have been 1,400 incidents in and adjacent to the DMZ, resulting in the deaths of 899 North Koreans, 394 South Koreans, and ninety American soldiers.[5] Major North-South operations included commando attacks on the Seoul Presidential Blue House in 1968, an assassination attempt on President Park Chung Hee in 1974 (his wife was killed), the murder of half the South Korean cabinet in a bomb blast in Rangoon, Burma, in 1983, and periodic naval clashes. South Korea has no illusions about its northern neighbor, but after more than half a century of tragic confrontation, under the Kim Dae Jung presidency it broke decisively with the half-century old Cold War confrontation and staked its future on a "Sunshine" policy. South Koreans are well aware that there have been acts of terror on their side of the DMZ until very recently and have a deep sense that the problems of North Korea are rooted in the division system itself, not in any intrinsic North Korean evil. They are therefore much less inclined to issue moralistic denunciations of the North than is the United States. Many in the South hold to an optimistic scenario for the future that sees the human rights and other problems of contemporary North Korea being resolved by popular protest and pressure, as they were in South Korea, rather than by outside intervention, or worse, by the cataclysm of renewed war.

Recent global outpourings of analysis and commentary on the "Korean problem" tend to be characterized by righteous indignation over North Korea's acts and pronouncements, but they are also, consciously or unconsciously, and in ways we hardly notice characterized by an "imperial" frame of reference. Insistence that Pyongyang submit to the will of the "international community" often means that it must submit to the will of Washington. To the extent that one adopts an alternative, Korean, frame of reference and a Seoul-centered approach, the problem begins to look quite different. Nobody understands North Korea better, is in the present climate more positive and encouraging about dealing with it, and has more to lose from getting it wrong than the government and people of South Korea.

Although whatever threat North Korea might pose would above all be a threat to the South, people there seem remarkably relaxed about it. While not ignoring the military threat, both at a governmental and at a popular level, the main focus instead is on the need to help Pyongyang deal with its economic, security, and diplomatic problems. North Korea's possible political and social collapse threatens the South as much as any missile. The disruption caused already by the steady stream of refugees across the Tumen and Yalu rivers into China would be nothing compared to the chaos that would ensue in both South Korea and China if Kim's regime were actually to collapse, sending millions of desperate people fleeing on foot into China or into the South, or by boat across the Sea of Japan and the Yellow Sea to Japan and China. The region, but especially Seoul, would then face a vast humanitarian catastrophe, exacerbated by the difficulty of controlling nuclear and other materials in the confusion. Induced collapse through the application of sanctions could create a social and economic nightmare for the South, leaving it with twenty-two million starving people on its borders, not to speak of an army of hundreds of thousands of troops just across the border that could spin out of control. During the Cold War, Seoul hoped and planned for the day when it would take over the North. But after careful study of the process of German unification, officials in Seoul came to understand that "shock" reunification would cost up to $3,200 billion and would be likely to drag the South's economy into recession, if not depression, threatening the entire northeast Asian region.[6] So Seoul reconsidered. "Sunshine," the announced policy of Kim Dae Jung, was the outcome.

## "SUNSHINE"

As a policy, "Sunshine" implies reunification postponed. Gradual reform, accommodation, and cooperation replace it, leaving reunification to some future date. In the interim, Seoul concentrates on trying to understand the complex crisis Pyongyang faces and on taking steps to prevent, rather than accelerate, its collapse. Pyongyang's engagement in bilateral and multilateral forums is to be encouraged, as are international guarantees of its security so that it can lower its levels of militarization. As Lim Dong Woon, a senior advisor to South Korean president Roh, put it, the North Korean problem will only be resolved "when the country suspected of building nuclear weapons doesn't feel any security threats and is able to build relationships of trust with other countries."[7] South Korea therefore aims to "create an environment in which North Korea will feel secure without nuclear weapons."[8] The South's differences with Washington are not over long-term, strategic objectives, but over tactics. For, unlike the Bush administration, Seoul rules out the use of force.

A war on the Korean peninsula between the United States and North Korea is virtually impossible if South Korea says "no." During the crisis of 1994, when an American air assault was avoided only at the last minute, then-president Kim Young

Sam summoned U.S. ambassador James Laney to tell him that he would not move even a single one of South Korea's 650,000 troops to back the United States in case a war broke out because of the bombing of the Yongbyon reactor. He then telephoned President Clinton and spoke to him for thirty-two minutes, telling him, "There would be no inter-Korean war while I was the president . . . I criticized the United States for planning to stage a war on our land."[9] The American commanding general, Gary Luck, told a congressional committee after the crisis had eased that he had calculated a million people might die, including 80,000 to 100,000 Americans.[10] During his presidency, Kim Dae Jung made it plain that he held even more strongly to the view of his predecessor. When he met George W. Bush in February 2002, he reminded him of that 1994 Pentagon assessment of the astronomical casualties that war would entail.[11]

In February 2003, a new president, Roh Moo-Hyun, took over. The fifth son of a poor farmer whose formal education ended after vocational high school, Roh educated himself to pass the country's notoriously difficult bar examination. He then became a renowned human rights lawyer and a leading figure in the struggles that led to the democratic revolution of 1987. During his presidential campaign, Roh insisted, "I don't believe the problem can be solved by pressuring North Korea."[12] If elected, he swore he would not kowtow to Washington or support the imposition of a deadline on Pyongyang to comply with international demands to end its nuclear program. If necessary, he added, he would "guarantee North Korea's security."[13] During 2003, however, as the pressures from Washington mounted, Roh adopted a more ambiguous posture, going out of his way to appear cooperative when meeting with George Bush in April, subsequently committing a small 700-man, noncombat unit of South Korean troops to the occupation of Iraq, and late in 2003 giving serious consideration to the commitment of a more substantial, brigade-strength, combat unit of around 5,000 men. That decision would be based, according to Youn Young-kwan, the South Korean foreign minister, on "cost versus profit, moral justification, public opinion and the international situation."[14] Plainly public Korean opinion was against any dispatch of troops without a UN mandate, and the main consideration in the government's thinking was to placate Washington in order to preserve some influence with it in the ongoing negotiations over North Korea and to avoid the sort of pressures that threatened to send its economy into a tailspin.

Where Washington looks at North Korea and sees a nuclear threat, Seoul sees desperate poverty and misery. It is inclined more to pity than to fear by the spectacle of fellow countrymen hungry, desperate, and oppressed, "trapped by the ironies of the end of the Cold War and by the harshness of the Kim Jong Il regime, but also being pushed into a dangerous corner by the . . . Americans."[15] The consensus among the defense authorities in Seoul is that no North Korean attack is planned or likely. Whatever threat exists has existed for fifty years. If Pyongyang wanted to destroy Seoul, and in return be promptly annihilated, it could do so at any time, but people in Seoul see little reason to judge the North Korean authorities insane. Instead, they see a porcupine stiffening its bristles in the face of external threats.

They know that the North Korean army, supposedly the world's fifth-largest in size, is dilapidated and antiquated. Its conventional weapons include over 3,000 tanks, 11,000 artillery pieces, 850 combat aircraft, and 430 combat ships, but much of this equipment is vintage 1960s (some even 1950s), and the military suffers an acute shortage of fuel (which could be totally cut off any time that China chose). The Iraq War of 2003 showed how useless even 1980s equipment was against hi-tech American forces. North Korea's could hardly do better.

As for North Korean airpower, those who scan North Korean skies report that hardly anything ever moves in them. Some fighter pilots get ten hours a year in flight training, others virtually none. In the United States a fighter pilot gets around 210 hours of flight training, in Israel about 180, and in the Japanese Self-Defense Forces about 160.[16] That means that North Korean pilots cannot be confident of doing much but taking off and landing, and their ability to defend North Korean skies would surely not last five minutes if challenged. The very thought of the military colossus that accounts for 40 percent of global military spending going to war with one of the poorest and most depressed countries on earth is obscene, yet there are undoubtedly powerful figures in Washington who contemplate, even urge, it. "We crushed the Iraqi Republican Guard," says Richard Perle, until recently of the influential Defense Policy Board in Washington, "and we can do likewise with the North Korean army."[17]

What people in Seoul fear is what Pyongyang fears: a preemptive U.S. attack. They know that in North Korea, for the army as for everybody, food is the major preoccupation. There may be over a million soldiers (1.17 million is the official figure), and they enjoy an undoubted priority in the distribution of resources. But, while nominally better off than others, many are still malnourished. Reports from defectors refer to internal studies showing the average weight of soldiers to be only 110 pounds (50 kgs).[18] Over the past year, military parades have been canceled; there have been virtually no reports of maneuvers or exercises, hardly any movement even of trucks, much less signs of mobilization for war; and since the country is regularly scanned from the skies and its military communications are monitored by American (and other) intelligence services, there can be few secrets when it comes to national military preparedness. Some units are undoubtedly highly trained and probably highly motivated, but they are likely to be a minority. Others have set themselves up in businesses. They run mines or trading companies or fisheries in order to sustain themselves. A well-informed source estimates that many soldiers, perhaps as many as nine out of ten, "have little more than militia training and are generally employed most of the time in agriculture."[19] When special orders are issued that "soldiers should never, no matter how hungry they are, steal food from a farm," or recruits are told "your body may freeze from hunger and cold . . . but you need to train your mind to tolerate such circumstances" we can surmise that the plunder of farms is a serious problem and that recruits can expect to starve and freeze.[20]

North Korea, as Washington constantly stresses, also has missiles—certainly short- and medium-range ones, and it may be on the way to producing long-range, intercontinental ones. That sounds threatening, but the threat begins to weaken once one considers the practical realities surrounding this arsenal. When some short-range, conventional "land to ship" cruise missiles were fired into adjacent seas early in 2003, after due notice, the event resulted in front-page headlines around the world. The United States responded by dispatching twenty-four long-distance B-1 and B-52 bombers to Guam ("in case they might be needed in Korea"); six F117 Nighthawk Stealth fighters and F15E Strike Eagles were left in Korea following joint exercises held with the South Korean military (for the first time in a decade); the aircraft carrier *Carl Vinson* was dispatched to Japanese waters, and regular spy flights were also stepped up.[21] What would happen if North Korea were to test-fire anything of greater range can only be imagined.

As for the medium-range *Nodong* missiles, although they are seen as a serious threat in Japan, for South Koreans they do not add greatly to the destructive potential of the estimated 12,000 conventional artillery pieces dug into the hills above the DMZ. A chemical or biological payload would, of course, change all this, and North Korea is thought to possess both but to be unlikely to consider using either unless facing extermination. Tested only once, in May 1993, the *Nodong* flew 500 kms into the Sea of Japan. It has not flown since, although further tests were conducted by Pakistan and Iran, only one of which was successful.[22] Satellite photographs of the test site showed a "shed, a dirt road, a launch pad and a rice paddy."[23] No paved roads or rail-link to it exists; nobody even lives at the site for much of the year; and it has no industrial support or other test facilities. The Federation of American Scientists concluded that "this facility was not intended to support, and in many respects is incapable of supporting, the extensive test program that would be needed to fully develop a reliable missile system."[24] Although the 1998 Rumsfeld Report of the Commission to Assess the Ballistic Missile Threat to the United States concluded that North Korea had a sizable missile production infrastructure and that it was "highly likely that considerable numbers of Nodongs have been produced," what strikes American scientists as most remarkable about the *Nodong* is "the disparity between the extremely modest and protracted North Korean test activities and the vast scale of the American response to this program."[25] John Pike of the Federation of American Scientists describes it as "the mouse that roared." A serious program designed to build nuclear warhead–carrying missiles would require continuous testing, whereas Pyongyang has had "just two ineffectual launches—both out of pique at U.S. reluctance to negotiate."[26]

American intelligence estimates put the capacity of the *Nodong*—which in 1993 only flew 500 kms—at about 1,000 kms, and then, without evidence of further testing, raised that to 1,300 kms, bringing much more of Japan within its potential range. The estimate of *Nodong* numbers also mysteriously doubled, and then doubled again. U.S. and South Korean estimates to 1999 were of nine or ten mobile launchers and deployable missiles,[27] but that number grew magically to 100 and then 200.[28] How many of them there really are, and how far they could fly and how accurately they could be directed, nobody knows. The U.S. manufacturers and distributors of the Patriot and other missile defense systems undoubtedly owe a huge debt to Kim Jong Il's struggling scientists. Their efforts have been crucial to persuading governments in the United States, Japan, possibly South Korea, and even Australia to invest countless billions of dollars in the coming years in missile defense systems. For two missile launches in ten years, one of them a failure, this is an impressive record.

So far as the accuracy of the *Nodong* is concerned, Japanese military affairs analyst Eya Osamu calculates that one in two *Nodongs* might land within 2.5 kilometers of its target.[29] Others estimate that a *Nodong* attack might produce an effect something like the German V-2 rocket attacks on London during the Blitz, a good deal of fear and some buildings destroyed, but nothing like the blood-curdling "sea of fire" occasionally threatened by the North's spokesmen and its press. However, the Japanese government takes the missile issue very seriously indeed. The Japan Defense Agency, the equivalent of the Pentagon, calculates that fifty *Nodong* missiles, loaded with chemical warheads, might cause up to 4 million casualties in Seoul and comparable devastation in Tokyo.[30] A military specialist from the Brookings Institution looks to a "very optimistic scenario" involving "tens of thousands of dead Koreans . . . and probably several thousand dead Americans" in a missile attack. "Optimistic" presumably means casualty figures in the thousands rather than the millions.[31]

Pyongyang's only other "missile" test was a failed 1998 attempt to lift a satellite into orbit. The vehicle seems to have blown up in flight, although not before passing over Japan. The untested *Taepodong* would be the military version of the same missile. Its range was initially assessed at 1,500 to 2,200 kms, but that too has steadily grown. The December 2001 National

Intelligence Estimates projected that an upgraded version of *Taedopong* "could deliver a several-hundred-pound payload up to 10,000 kms," sufficient to strike not only anywhere in Japan or Alaska, but "parts of the continental United States."[32] These technical estimates are based, it must be said, on extraordinary confidence in North Korea's scientific and engineering skills, scarcely warranted by the fact that the single test of this missile was a failure. Preparations for launching of a *Taepodong-2*, as it is known, were detected in 1999 but then suspended, and there has been no sign of significant activity at the site since. If ever the *Taepodong-2* were launched all that could be said for certainty is that all hell would break loose. Untested, its flight would be unpredictable, but its launch, perhaps even just signs of preparations for its launch, would almost certainly trigger the threat of massive U.S. military intervention and possibly a Japanese military response as well, since Japan's defense minister has said that evidence of a missile being readied for launch would be enough to warrant attack. It may be that there are those in Washington or Tokyo who hope to goad North Korea into precisely such a move, something that could then be used to justify an attack.

While neoconservative Washington sees Pyongyang as "evil" incarnate, a regime with which there can be no compromise, and dismisses Seoul's "Sunshine" as either a hopeless and worthless policy or, worse, dangerous appeasement, South-North engagement continues on a wide range of economic, cultural, sporting, and transport fronts. Years of "Sunshine" and multiple layers of contact and negotiation have even begun to thaw the long-frozen Demilitarized Zone that divides North and South. Seoul's "sunshine" is slowly accomplishing something once thought impossible: the restoration of a measure of trust between North and South, one Korea and the other. Delegations are entertained and contracts signed and implemented, fear diminishes, and confidence grows.

## "LOVE HIM OR HATE HIM"

As time passes, the gap widens between the thinking of the United States as the global hyperpower, reliant as it is on massive force projection capacity, and of South Korea as a small Asian country still struggling to achieve national unification with the North, heal the wounds of civil war, and establish the modest goals of peace and development. Like his predecessor, Kim Dae Jung, Roh Moo-Hyun is a pragmatist, committed to continuation of the "Sunshine" policy as the best chance of easing tensions on the peninsula, resolving the nuclear question, and advancing the goal of eventual North-South unification. While Washington urges Tokyo, Moscow, Beijing, even Canberra, to pressure Pyongyang into nuclear disarmament, it is reluctant to have Seoul play any central role in the diplomatic process. Despite its efforts to persuade Washington that it is "on side" in the process of persuading North Korea to abandon its nuclear programs, Seoul is unable to overcome the suspicion that it is too soft on its compatriots or even that some members of its administration might be using "back-door" channels of communication with Pyongyang to undermine the United States. As Richard Allen, formerly national security adviser under the Reagan administration and now close associate of Donald Rumsfeld has put it, South Korea "must decide whether to side with North Korea or with the US."[33]

Yet as cross-border relationships deepen, the South displays increasing confidence about dealing with Pyongyang. While the United States enjoyed cozy relationships with the dictators in the South until 1987 (sharing with them the vision of someday conquering North Korea), the more democratic the country has become the more troublesome to Washington it has seemed. From the top to the bottom of society, South Korean confidence in the United States is diminishing and readiness to support compromise deals with North Korea is growing, so that Seoul threatens to become almost as much of a thorn in U.S. plans for regional and global order as Pyongyang. Following the election of Roh in 2002, senior American officials rushed to Seoul to "speed up bilateral policy coordination" (as the conservative Japanese conservative newspaper, the *Yomiuri* delicately put it), meaning to bring the new government in line with Washington's policy desires.[34] Meetings of the Trilateral Coordination and Oversight Group, which involves the U.S., Japanese, and South Korean governments, have had the same purpose: to "contain" Seoul and rein in its Sunshine fantasies.[35] When Deputy Secretary of State Richard Armitage visited Seoul that same month as part of the process, he was disconcerted to find the government there far less interested in talk of war than in securing a revision of the Status of Forces Agreement to make American servicemen subject to South Korean law, so that in future they could be disciplined and punished locally.[36]

Not only do Korean governments now almost automatically distance themselves from Washington's hard-line, but anti-American demonstrations draw large crowds and opinion surveys show that the United States is less liked there than anywhere in east Asia (or, for that matter, Europe). The Koreans who elected Roh as president in 2002 are sometimes described as the "386" generation, born in the 1960s, educated in the 1980s, and now in their thirties or early 40s. This is the generation that fought for democracy against U.S.–supported military regimes until 1987 and in the process learned to distrust whatever the government told them about North Korea. Nowadays, half of South Koreans profess to "dislike" or hold negative views of the United States.[37] Gallup polls show nearly 60 percent of them no longer believe North Korea poses a security threat, and a majority believe that Pyongyang is sincere in its efforts toward reunification.[38] A BBC poll in mid-2003 found that 48 percent of South Koreans saw the United States as a greater threat to world peace than North Korea.[39] Other polls indicate that between 60 and 70 percent of Southerners no longer see North Korea as a threat, favor normalization, and oppose U.S. attempts at "containment."[40] Only 31 percent support cooperation with the United States.[41] In the depths of the standoff between North Korea and the United States in the summer of 2003, Seoul's *Joongang Daily* reported that only 9 percent of South Koreans believed the North's nuclear threat should be a major government concern.[42] For a supposedly close and strategically crucial ally, these are remarkable figures. Outrage late in 2002 was especially strong following the acquittal by an American military court of two soldiers accused of negligent homicide in the deaths of two young girls. Roh became president because he was seen to represent the views of a majority of his countrymen. On March 1, 2003, Seoul hosted, for the first time, a joint South-North ceremony to commemorate the eighty-fourth anniversary of the *Samil* movement, a peaceful uprising for national independence brutally crushed by Japan in 1919. This strengthening sense of a shared past and a common identity opens up the possibility of sharing dreams for the future.

South Korea's President Roh is, however, in the eye of the storm, caught between immensely powerful pressures, on the one hand from Washington, and on the other from the members of the 386 generation that want an increased Korean autonomy. Faced with Washington's demands for a substantial Korean contingent to be sent to Iraq to support the American occupation and for a transformation of the role of U.S. forces in Korea from narrowly defensive to broadly strategic in support of U.S. security policy in northeast Asia as a whole (in the region bounded by Hokkaido, Taiwan, and Guam), Roh vacillated. Showing one face to his domestic supporters and another to his foreign allies, his support plummeted from 80 percent to 20 percent and in October 2003, after only nine months in office, he took the dramatic decision to conduct a December plebiscite to test his popularity.[43] The outcome of this unprecedented ploy was impossible to predict, but South Korea's voice, at least temporarily, is likely to be weakened by the intense and complicated diplomatic maneuvering over North Korea that was underway.

Despite this confusion, it is hard to avoid the impression that the passions of war and Cold War have largely burned themselves out in South Korea. Security is not neglected, but both governmental and nongovernmental think tanks focus their attention on economic challenges and particularly on how to help North Korea stave off collapse. The state-funded Korea Development Institute has a blueprint for generating a 7-percent annual growth rate in the North to raise per capita income, feed the population, and attract the foreign capital necessary to rebuild its economic infrastructure.[44] Outside government circles, some of these responsible for hauling South Korea out of abject poverty only four decades ago now offer suggestions to Pyongyang on how it might do likewise. Having played a key role in the Cold War confrontation on the Korea peninsula, O Wonchol, right-hand man to dictator Park Chung Hee in the 1960s and 1970s and one of the principal architects of South Korea's industrial transformation, now seeks ways to help Pyongyang "normalize" and develop. Pragmatism and confidence that the North is not lunatic or beyond redemption characterize such an approach.

The challenge for North Korean leader Kim Jong Il, wrote O in the monthly magazine *Wolgan Chosun*, is to become the North Korean equivalent of the Chinese leader Deng Xiaoping who in the postwar era moved his country into a burst of capitalist development. If Kim would learn from the experiences of both South Korea and China, adopt an export-oriented economic system in place of the current *Juche* policies of economic autarchy, and launch an all-out development drive, the prospects could be quite bright. Knowing that in 1999 Kim

Jong Il expressed to Hyundai founder Chung Ju-yung his admiration for South Korea's modernizing dictator, Park Chung Hee, O recommends that the North Korean dictator do what Park did: empower the country's best technocratic brains to form a "staff headquarters" and lead an export revolution. The conditions for industrialization in North Korea, he points out, are favorable: All land is state-owned, labor is cheap and of high quality, minerals abound, and educational levels are high.

A million engineers and technicians should be dispatched abroad (many to South Korea, as part of a necessary peninsula-wide reshuffling of labor and resources), thus generating immediate revenues. Most existing industrial plant, already obsolete, should simply be scrapped. The Rajin-Sonbong area on the Sino-Russian border should shift its focus from light to heavy and chemical-oriented industry, and a deep-water port should be dredged to service it. Industrial plant in some sectors should simply be moved from South to North, one immediate candidate being the South's surplus coal briquette factories, thereby solving the North's heating problems and arresting chronic deforestation due to the need for firewood. However, O recognizes that a precondition for success must be a normalization of relations with South Korea as well as with the United States and Japan, opening the path to low-interest international development funds from the Asia Development Bank and World Bank.

## The Family Business

Building on the industrialization experience of the Park years and the democratization and internationalization of later presidencies, Seoul could offer a distinctive, Korea-centered vision. One scholar goes so far as to suggest a South Korean "protectorate" over the North in the realm of national security, and foreign policy might be a possible first step in a multistage process of peaceful transition to a unified Korean state.

Alexandre Mansourov writes:

> Only the South has to take the North Korean demands
> seriously and, in turn, can guarantee the North's security
> and assist in economic development. The only sacrifice the
> North will have to make is to accept some practical limita-
> tions on its sovereignty, including in such strategic areas as
> WMD development . . . After all, if Korea is indeed one, as
> Koreans like to stress, it is all one nation, one family busi-
> ness.[45]

The word *protectorate* has negative and ill-omened historical
associations in the Korean context, but the general thrust of his
argument—the desirability, on the "Korea problem," of substi-
tuting a Seoul-Pyongyang framework of thinking for the
present Washington-Pyongyang one—makes good sense.
Koreans themselves—North, South, and overseas—will have to
come up with some more historically sensitive formula that
reflects legitimate concerns over face, history, and "correct"
relationships, so that through a deepening of North-South con-
versation and cooperation "Korea" can find a voice with which
to address the world. The challenge for Seoul now is to build a
buffer of protection and a bridge of communication linking
Pyongyang to that world, while guaranteeing that international
obligations are met and ensuring Pyongyang's legitimate security concerns; the task ahead for the government in Seoul is
nothing less than internationalizing "Sunshine."

The best hope for a way out of the impasse is not likely to
be pressure exerted through some combination of "Five plus
Two" (the Security Council's five permanent members plus
Japan and South Korea), "Five plus Five" (the Security
Council's five plus South Korea, North Korea, Japan, Australia,
and the European Union), or even the "Six-Side" formula
(North and South Korea, the United States, China, Russia, and

Japan) that became the forum for negotiating on North Korea's nuclear threat from mid-2003, but a deepening of the accommodation between Pyongyang and Seoul, based on a simple formula of "One plus One equals One." However mathematically unorthodox, such a formula holds an essential truth that Koreans at least recognize. With such a connection, a combination of fraternal trust and memories of the disastrous consequences caused by reliance on the intervention of powerful outsiders may still combine to point a path forward.

The situation today on the Korean peninsula resembles the situation one hundred years ago. Modern Korean nationalism, frustrated by foreign intervention for over a century, remains a powerful force, and beneath the state structures of North and South lies a shared Korean-ness. From the Korean standpoint, whether in Pyongyang or Seoul, the issue is one of *Sadae* (reliance on powerful friends and neighbors) versus *Juche* (self-reliance). One hundred years ago, and at successive moments since, many thought it wisest to look toward great and powerful neighbors. That mindset undergirded a century of colonial subjugation, national division, and catastrophic, internecine bloodshed. Facing unprecedented crisis now, South and North Korea have to find some way to trust each other more than they trust any of the great powers that surround them. The stakes are even higher than they were a century ago, for this time the peninsula itself, and all of its people, are at risk. The *Juche* that Kim Il Sung embraced a half-century ago was soon turned into an illiberal, statist ideology in which autonomy was reserved only for the leader, but the aspiration remains and continues to have a strong Korean resonance. There should still be room for a distinctive Korean ideology that emphasized a united country, national autonomy, regional cooperation on an equal basis with neighbor states, and the moral autonomy of citizens.

Japan's choices in the present North Korean crisis will have

# JAPAN AND NORTH KOREA:
# DIFFICULT NEIGHBORS

much to do with determining its future and its identity, not to speak of its role in the region and the world. Two incidents from 2003 highlight the strange and tangled relationship between the two neighbor states, one a global economic superpower, the other bankrupt, isolated, and almost universally reviled.

On August 25, a North Korean ship, carrying passengers and freight on the sole regular route of communication between North Korea and Japan, entered Niigata harbor on Japan's northwest coast. On hand to receive it were 1,500 police, 400 officials of various ministries connected with trade and shipping, at least 300 media representatives (some in helicopters or on motor boats), 400-odd rightists in their characteristic black wagons shouting nationalist or anti-North Korean slogans and abuse, and a large crowd representing the association of families of those abducted by North Korea in the 1970s and 1980s. The whole country watched the spectacle on television. Just weeks earlier, hooded witnesses had told a Washington congressional committee that the ship was a conduit for crucial missile parts to North Korea and for narcotics from it. The most thorough of searches by the mass of officials turned up nothing but a minor infringement of the rules, however, and the ship sailed off again the next day.

Two weeks later, a time bomb was delivered to the Tokyo home of a senior foreign ministry official who had been involved in intensive negotiations with North Korea. A group declaring its mission to "punish traitors" claimed responsibility, the bomb was intercepted, and nobody was hurt. On hearing of the attack, Tokyo's hugely popular governor, Ishihara Shintaro, declared that the official in question had got what he deserved. The following day, he amplified his comments, adding that while he had not meant to endorse the planting of bombs, he thought there were good reasons for targeting this particular official, who was a traitor worthy of death ten times over. Politicians and editorialists made various critical or dissenting statements, but Ishihara's prestige and popularity suffered not the slightest dent. No serious move was made to treat his statement as what it plainly was: an incitement to terror.[1]

These two incidents point to the vein of anger, frustration, even hatred for North Korea, and anybody thought to be on its side, that throbs just beneath the surface of everyday life in contemporary Japan. It is not that North Korea has not given cause for offense, but that the Japanese response is so immoderate and so lacking in any element of reflection why there is the problem, let alone any sense of responsibility for it. The anger at public officials and the language of punishing traitors were both reminiscent of the mood of early 1930s Japan, when fascism was already in the wings. Though the foreign ministry official escaped the violence directed at him, threats, and occasionally actual attacks, against North Korean offices and institutions in Japan have risen sharply, and children at Korean schools in Japan report steadily rising levels of violence directed at them, sometimes in the form of abuse but sometimes of physical assault, their distinctive Korean clothes being slashed while they walk in the streets or travel in subways.[2] In the late nineteenth century, as today, the Korean peninsula had a special importance for Japan. Then, as today's, the terms and conditions of Japan's relationship to the region and the world were at issue. Then, Japan chose to build an Asian empire and craft an ideology of "Asianism" under the guidance or leadership of Japan, which therefore became both "non-Asian" and "super-Asian." Korea became the crucial foothold for expansion as Japan evolved into an imperial power and participated in the European carve-up of Asia. Victories in two wars, against imperial China and czarist Russia, did in fact establish it as a major imperialist power. From the perspective of the twentieth century, however, these were disastrous victories, setting up the irreconcilable contradictions between Japan and its neighbors in the region that were finally resolved only when the empire collapsed in 1945.

Korea was both the victim and the spoils of Japan's rise, core of its empire, focus of its prejudice and fear. From Korea, Japan appropriated land, wealth, history, even family names, language, and identity, imposing in its stead its own national identity, religion, and emperor system on a reluctant people. In 1923, when Tokyo was struck by a devastating earthquake, panic and fear turned the people of that city against the "outsider" Koreans in their midst. When rumors spread that "the Koreans" were poised to attack, or were poisoning the wells, gangs of vigilantes took to the streets, slaughtering over 6,000 Koreans in a horrendous massacre still to be officially investigated. In the final stages of the empire, hundreds of thousands of young Koreans were sent either to Japan itself or throughout the empire as soldiers, prison camp guards, laborers, and, in the most tragic case of all sex slaves for the Imperial Japanese Army. In repeated cases before the Japanese courts, they have been denied compensation.

In the nineteenth and early twentieth centuries, Japan, like all imperial powers, failed to see or understand the rise of nationalism or to grasp what an impossible task it would be in the long term to hold together an empire by force. Though the empire was dissolved in 1945, Japan remained blocked from reconciliation with its neighbor region, first by the U.S. occupation and then by the Cold War. Swathed in the embrace of its powerful cross-Pacific ally, it tended to continue looking at "Asia" as separate, distant, and secondary. For two decades after 1945 Japan studiously avoided having anything to do with either of its Korean neighbors. Then in 1965, under pressure from Washington for Cold War reasons, it "normalized" relations with South Korea, though offering no apologies for the crimes and horrors of the colonial era or any compensation to its victims. Under circumstances of continuing distrust, resentment only slowly dissipated. By the time of the Kim Dae Jung presidency in 1998 and especially of the Soccer World Cup of 2002 (sponsored jointly and played equally in both countries), it was possible for the first time to see warmth, spontaneity, and mutual respect in the bilateral relationship. For North Korea, however, four decades of colonial rule were followed by nearly six decades of unbroken hostility and confrontation.

In Korea, there is an even deeper layer of history, alive in popular memory for more than 400 years because it was never assuaged. Japan has neither recognized nor apologized for the depredations of its late sixteenth century invasion of Korea, instead tending to celebrate it and to grant hero status to Toyotomi Hideyoshi, the man who led the Japanese forces. Korean culture was at that time in many, perhaps most, respects save warfare, more developed than Japan's and the peninsula was plundered mercilessly by the 160,000-man strong Japanese force, which seized and carried off not only potters but also doctors, printers, artisans in wood and metal, paper makers, scroll makers, painters, dyers, weavers and spinners, garden designers and experts, scholars, large numbers of young women, many cultural treasures, and printing presses—the "high-tech" items of their time—while also selling many Koreans as slaves or exchanging them for guns or silk. Where Japanese tend to forget these matters, Korean memories are long. The Korean terms of abuse used to refer to Japanese today date from this dark period. True "normalization" would call not only for significant adjustments on the part of North Korea to the modern world, but also for significant adjustments in the way Japanese collective memory is constructed.

As the twenty-first century began, the Japanese media was filled to overflowing with negative news about North Korea— missiles, abductions, nuclear weapons, narcotics, and spy ships. In Japanese understanding, North Korea was a black hole threatening to suck the region into chaos for utterly incomprehensible reasons. The background to the peculiar history and mentality of North Korea, and particularly Japan's place in that history, was rarely understood. Instead North Korea was simply presented as a mad, perverse, or ill place.

## The Summit of Apology: Pyongyang, September 17, 2002

Pyongyang had to normalize relations with Japan for all sorts of reasons—to stave off American pressure and to secure relief from its economic plight, among other desperate needs. Following sporadic exploratory talks during the preceding decade and a more intensive series of exchanges in the preceding year, a tentative framework for agreement was drawn up. It amounted to a signpost toward normalization. For Pyongyang, the outstanding issue was its demand for apologies and reparations for the crimes of Japanese colonialism; for Tokyo, the encroachment of North Korean spy ships into Japanese waters and the suspicion that a dozen or so of its nationals in earlier decades had been abducted by agents of North Korea.

The visit of Japanese Prime Minister Koizumi to Pyongyang on September 17, 2002, held the promise of a great historic reconciliation. However, within days, Japanese hostility, rekindled, was surging to new heights, with prominent figures calling for severing rather than normalizing the tenuous relationship between the two countries, or even for making pre-emptive military strikes against it.

The September meeting between the Japanese and North Korean leaders was tense, short (a single afternoon), and dramatic. Koizumi reportedly took with him to Pyongyang his own bento lunchbox and then brought it back to Tokyo that night, unopened. It is hard to think of any summit where the main agenda on both sides was apology. The two leaders did not sit down to eat or drink together, and on both sides the "apologies" themselves were strained, formulaic, and of doubtful sincerity. Koizumi expressed "deep remorse and heartfelt apology" for "the tremendous damage and suffering" inflicted on the people of Korea during the colonial era, while Kim Jong Il apologized for the abductions of thirteen Japanese between 1977 and 1982 and for the dispatch of spy ships into Japanese waters.

Japan had long resisted any claim for the reparations that might properly have been expected to accompany any "heartfelt apology" and only came to the table with Pyongyang when assured that the demand for reparations would be dropped. The wording of the declaration—virtually identical to that used in the Japanese–South Korean talks in October 1998—was acceptable to the Tokyo bureaucracy precisely because it carried no legal implications. Once issued it was completely forgotten in Tokyo and ignored by the Japanese media. The "harm" caused by Japan over thirty-five years of colonial rule was as nothing compared to the harm done to Japan in more recent decades.

In Japanese ruling Liberal-Democratic Party circles, normalization, it was calculated, would lead to substantial "aid and development" programs and would therefore open lucrative business opportunities for core factions of the Party in the future construction of roads, bridges, dams, power stations, railways, and other elements of a North Korean infrastructure, to the benefit of their associates in the recession-hit construction industry. Significant funds had been creamed off such deals by the ruling faction in the sixties, when relations were first normalized with South Korea. A similar prospect almost certainly attracted the embattled stalwarts of Japan's construction state. The system of collusive and corrupt links between bureaucrats, politicians, and construction sector businesses that, since the 1970s, succeeded in stuffing the country with unnecessary "public works" and burdening it with astronomical levels of debt, is known as the *doken kokka*, or "construction state." North Korea undoubtedly needs large-scale infrastructural works to modernize the country, but it also represents virgin territory of almost unlimited potential for Japan's *doken kokka*.[3]

Despite reservations, especially over having to abandon the compensation claim, for Pyongyang the urgency of the need for economic reconstruction was compelling. Colonial-era issues would have to be settled only indirectly in order to achieve normalization of relations with Japan.[4] Kim Jong Il also had to abandon his long-held insistence that the Japanese colonial regime was an illegal imposition, maintained by military force, and yield to the Japanese view that it was properly constituted under international law. It was the same bitter climb-down that had been forced on South Korea as the price of its normalization with Japan in 1965. Many in South Korea lamented this as yet another opportunity lost for Korea as a whole to correct the historical record.[5]

Kim also made two apologies. He admitted to the abduction between 1977 and 1982 of a group of Japanese civilians, among them a schoolgirl, a beautician, a cook, three dating couples (whisked away from remote beaches), and several students touring Europe. They had all been taken to Pyongyang either to teach Japanese-language courses to North Korean intelligence agents or so that their identities could be appropriated by North Korean agents operating in South Korea, Japan, or elsewhere. Insisting that he had no personal knowledge of all of this, Kim explained it in terms of "some elements of a special agency of state" having been "carried away by fanaticism and desire for glory."

Secondly, he explained and apologized for the incursions of so-called "mystery ships" into Japanese waters. Just a week before the Pyongyang meeting a "mystery ship," sunk after a brief gun battle in the East China Sea in December 2001, had been lifted from the seabed, so he had little choice but to say something about it. A Special Forces unit had been engaged in its own exercises, he claimed lamely, saying, "I had not imagined that it would go to such lengths and do such things . . . The Special Forces are a relic of the past and I want to take steps to wind them up."[6] On subsequent examination, the ship's North Korean origins were confirmed. It was found to have been armed to the teeth, with two antiaircraft missiles, two rocket launchers, a recoilless gun, twelve rockets, an antiaircraft gun, two light machine guns, three automatic rifles, and six grenades, as well as "an underwater scooter of a design rarely seen."[7] Though no evidence was found to suggest it had been involved in drugs, counterfeiting, smuggling, or other operations, it was plainly a ship up to no good.[8] The vessel was put on public display in Japan in May 2003.

Abduction and spying may be characterized as terrorist acts. There can be no justification for them, but history offers a context within which, at least, to understand them. "Normalcy" has not been known in the area of east Asia surrounding the Korean peninsula for a hundred years. Colonialism, division, war, Cold War, and unrelieved military confrontation have profoundly distorted not only the frame of state and interstate relationships, but also minds and souls.

Kim Jong Il's protests that he personally had been unaware of the spy ships or the abductions rang hollow, of course, because of his complete and unquestioned authority.[9] The organization most likely responsible for the abductions was thought to be something known as "Room 35," formerly the Overseas Intelligence Department of the Korean Workers' Party. Japanese government sources believe this same organization was responsible for a series of spectacular operations in the past, including the guerrilla attack on the Blue House, the South Korean presidential residence, in 1968; an October 1983 bomb attack in Rangoon, Burma, that killed seventeen members of a South Korean presidential delegation; and a November 1987 midair explosion that destroyed Korean Air Lines flight 859 over the Andaman Sea, killing all 115 people aboard. A separate "Section 56," under the ruling party's External Liaison Department, is suspected in the case of abductions from Europe.

Of the thirteen people abducted, Pyongyang admitted to having seized seven by force. Five, it claimed, went of their own free will, and another had been spirited away with help from a Japanese intermediary. Three weeks after the summit, the five who Pyongyang labeled the survivors returned to Japan in a special plane: two married couples, their children still in North Korea, who had been snatched when together on summer evening dates by the Japan Sea in 1978. With them was a woman who had been seized as a nineteen-year-old nurse with her mother on the island of Sado in the same year.

The "Pyongyang Five" returned to Tokyo on October 15, 2002, looking none the worse for wear after nearly twenty-five years and sporting the distinctive badges of loyalty to Kim Jong Il. The agreement between the two governments was that they would spend ten days to two weeks in Japan, after which, back in Pyongyang, their long-term future and that of their families would be worked out. Their refusal to speak ill of North Korea was seen as proof positive that they were unable to express themselves freely. Since it was inconceivable that they might have been living reasonably normal lives in North Korea, the explanation had to be that they had been "brainwashed." When they intimated after about a week that they preferred to return home early rather than waiting the full two weeks, a frenzied campaign began to restrain them. The mood of anguish, anger, and desire for revenge that stirred in Japan was comparable to what swept over the United States in the wake of September 11.

Dead were three couples and two individuals. The explanations of their fates offered by Pyongyang strained credulity. One couple, seized in 1978 from Kagoshima prefecture and married in North Korea, were said to have died between 1979 and 1981, both of heart failure; Yet the husband was aged then only 24 and his wife 27. He was said to have suffered his heart attack when swimming, but when the dates were checked in Japan it turned out that the Korean coast had been battered by a typhoon that day. A second couple, seized in 1978 and 1980 respectively and married in 1984, were said to have died within a week of each other in 1986, one of cirrhosis of the liver and the other in a traffic accident. A third couple, one seized in Spain in 1980, the other in Denmark in 1983 and married in North Korea in 1985, had died together, with a child, having been poisoned by a defective gas heater in 1988. The bodies of all of these victims had disappeared without trace, their remains washed away in floods, dam bursts, or landslides in the mid-1990s. A seventh casualty, abducted from Spain in 1980, supposedly died in a traffic accident in 1996, and his remains, too, were washed away by floods. However, Pyongyang reported that his remains had been recovered and reinterred in a common grave. When those remains were subject to DNA tests in Japan, however, they turned out to be those of a middle-aged woman. The eighth, and perhaps most poignant, case is that of the then thirteen-year-old schoolgirl, Yokota Megumi, seized on her way home from a badminton match in 1977. In 1986 she married a North Korean man, and a daughter, Hyegyong, was born the following year. According to Pyongyang's explanation, Yokota suffered from depression and committed suicide while undergoing treatment in 1983, when her daughter was just five years old.

Angry, disbelieving Japanese families of the victims denounced the documentation provided by Pyongyang as a travesty and insisted their loved ones must still be alive and should be brought back, if necessary "by force."[10] The Japanese National Police Agency now thinks that there may be more Japanese abductees than at first suspected, perhaps as many as forty.[11] There are also said to be abductees of various other nationalities (European, Arab, and Chinese), not to mention the approximately 500 citizens that South Korea claims have been abducted since 1953.[12] The attempt to gain international recognition for the North Korean film industry by abducting and coopting the services of South Korea's top director and leading lady was only the highest profile example of these.

Having admitted formal state responsibility for one set of criminal acts, Kim Jong Il immediately came under deeper suspicion for others, including the Rangoon bombing and the blowing-up of KAL 859. He presumably calculated that by giving up any "compensation" claims and by issuing his own confession, he would achieve a quick resolution of the abduction issue and then be able to move on to "normalization" and the raising of substantial economic cooperation funds. The figure of approximately ¥1.5 trillion (U.S. $12 billion) in "aid" was commonly cited as potentially on the table, roughly equivalent to the $500 million Japan paid to South Korea on the opening of that bilateral relationship.[13] Without question it would have been a lot of money for bankrupt North Korea, though it would only have amounted to slightly less than Japan's contribution to bankroll the Gulf War of 1991 or about as much as Tokyo's newest subway, the Oedo line. However, in the climate of deepening revulsion against North Korea that followed the Pyongyang meeting, the Japanese diet proved unwilling to appropriate a single yen in economic "cooperation" for Kim.

The apology was nonetheless unprecedented among communist or totalitarian states. Simply to have issued it, and in the process to have conceded so much to his old enemy, Japan, was itself evidence of Kim Jong Il's desperation. Had the talks yielded a dramatic improvement in North Korea's situation his decision to apologize might have been accepted as bold but necessary, but in fact it led to a sharp worsening of relations with Japan and the United States. It remains to be seen whether a regime so identified with the image of its ruler can survive such a loss of face on his part: the transformation of the semidivine "Dear Leader" into a flawed and hard-pressed politician who confesses to crimes—and to Japan, a former colonial master, no less.

Pyongyang and Tokyo showed similarly cavalier attitudes in the way they reported the historic encounter. In Pyongyang, Koizumi was said to have come to "meet the beloved general and apologize and make amends for the past." The talks were officially declared a triumph; nothing was said of the abductions, the spy ships, or Kim's apology.[14] In Tokyo, on the other hand, attention focused exclusively on the fact that the prime minister had forced an admission of guilt from a "disgraceful" state.[15] The question of whether Japan had evaded paying reparations to which Pyongyang had a moral or historical entitlement, or why the Japanese apology came fifty-seven years late, was ignored or attributed solely to the stubborn and unreasonable nature of the regime in the North.

## THE POLITICS OF OUTRAGE IN JAPAN

One irony, considering the subject at hand and the nature of apologies on all sides, was that during the era of colonial rule the Japanese had essentially kidnapped tens of thousands, if not hundreds of thousands, of Koreans to work under forced or near-forced conditions on the Japanese home islands, to be prostitutes ("comfort women") for the troops elsewhere in Asia during World War II; and to work in low-ranking jobs in the Japanese military such as guarding Western prisoners. This record has never been officially acknowledged, much less apologized for or compensated for. This was, for Koreans, North and South, the context within which the obviously criminal abductions of thirteen or more Japanese citizens were placed. For Koreans, the ensuing hubbub in Japan, during which the North Korean regime's abductions became quite literally the crime of the century and the Japanese ultimate victims of Asian brutality, had a painful air of unreality.

One Japanese commentator did catch some of this by questioning the normality of a Japan that

> invaded a neighboring country and turned it into a colony; appropriated people's land, names, language, towns and villages; killed those who resisted, forcibly abducting and dispatching around various war zones young men, as laborers and soldiers for the Imperial army, and women, as 'comfort women', at the cost of countless lives; and then, for fifty-seven years, did not apologize or make reparation.[16]

In Japan, however, after the summit all attention—especially the media spotlight—was obsessively focused on the abductees.

On October 24, the chief cabinet secretary, Fukuda Yasuo, announced that the five would not be allowed to go back to Pyongyang. The *Japan Times* spoke of the government's policy as something "essential . . . so that they can express their free will."[17] Under the headline "Allowed to Stay," the *Yomiuri* commented, "[T]he government will not allow them to return to North Korea, regardless of their intentions." George Orwell would have appreciated the slippery slope from the language of volition to the language of coercion, but few Japanese gave it passing thought. If coercion is freedom, then war is peace.

The drama of how the Pyongyang Five slowly "recovered" their Japaneseness was followed relentlessly by the national media. Television stations and print media gave the story blanket coverage. Their meetings with family or school friends, visits to hot spring resorts, every word they uttered, how much beer they did or did not drink, and what they sang for the karaoke were all scrutinized for inner meaning. The cohesion of the Japanese national family was celebrated by their return to the fold. The eventual casting off of their Kim Jong Il badges on December 19, 2002, was greeted with tears of national relief. On that day they announced their decision not to return to North Korea. At last, it seemed, they were Japanese again; they were free.

Japan not only refused to allow the "Five" to go back, but demanded the handover of their children by North Korea, their "return" to a country of which they knew nothing, irrespective of the fact that several of the "children" were now adults. Although the state saw the children as unquestionably "Japanese," five of them were still going about their lives in Pyongyang with no idea that their parents were Japanese, let alone originally abducted Japanese, or that they had been taken from them and would not be allowed to come home.[18] They had simply been deprived of their parents, without explanation, just as twenty and more years before, Japanese families had been deprived of their children. Only long after their parents' disappearance did these children learn, from North Korean authorities, that they were in Japan. Whether they know that they also are Japanese seems doubtful.

Evidently, before they even left for Pyongyang, Japanese officials had decided that the agreement on return would not be honored. Initially a "decision" taken by the Association of Families of Victims Kidnapped by North Korea, it was adopted by the government following intensive talks.[19] By its decision to keep the five permanently in Japan, the Japanese state not only reneged on its agreement on their return, but was in effect abducting them again.

What Tokyo referred to as the "free will" of the abductees actually meant the wishes of their families—that is to say their Japanese families, not their North Korean ones (since they now had both) and of radical activists and politicians pushing for Japan to fully militarize, develop nuclear weapons, and "get tough" with North Korea. The political influence of the various "support" groups has grown exponentially ever since the Japanese decision was made to cancel its agreement with Pyongyang over how the abductee matter would be resolved, thereby freezing relations with Pyongyang in place. North Korea policy merged with an orchestrated national campaign that had several objectives: to discredit and force the resignation of the ministry of foreign affairs bureaucrats who had negotiated the Pyongyang agreements in the first place; to revile any academics, media, or public figures who supported the agreements; to sever all ties with North Korea in order to force the overthrow of the Kim Jong Il regime; and to beef up Japan's military so that its policies could be implemented by force if necessary.

Nominally a group of organizations supporting the abductees, in fact the backers of this highly politicized campaign, probably reduced the likelihood of any early reunion of the families. The political figure who identified himself most closely with the campaign, Abe Shinzo, then deputy cabinet secretary, suggested that North Korea would be forced by its poverty and desperation to accept Japan's terms. "In Japan," he said, "there is food and there is oil, and since North Korea cannot survive the winter without them, it will crack before too long."[20] The key figure in the national campaign, Sato Katsumi, president of the Contemporary Korea Institute, was adamant that there could be no settlement with North Korea so long as the Kim Jong Il government remained in power. The mass-based movement of outright, at times semihysterical, hostility to North Korea that Abe, Sato, and others fanned diminished the likelihood of a positive Japanese role in seeking a peaceful resolution of the various disputes on the peninsula, including the nuclear one. During 2003, this group gathered strength and pressed its case on a receptive Washington and a reluctant Seoul. It became probably the most influential single pressure group in Japan, gaining three seats in the reorganized Koizumi cabinet of October 2003. Abe moved to the key post of secretary-general of the ruling Liberal-Democratic party and became the popular face of the "get tough with Pyongyang" public mood.

The conviction that Japan would have to teach North Korea how to be "a normal state" was widely shared. Starting in March 2003, a Japanese spy satellite, powered by essentially the same kind of rocket as North Korea's *Nodong* missiles, began scrutinizing North Korea from the skies. That such an act might be perceived as menacing in North Korea did not seem to be an issue in Japan.

The human turmoil of the sundered families, both of the abductees and their Japanese relatives as well as their Pyongyang families can only be guessed. Soga Hitomi, the former Sado Island nurse, had married former U.S. serviceman

Charles Jenkins two years after her arrival in North Korea and they had two teenage daughters. These two girls were in an the extremely difficult situation since their father was an American soldier who had disappeared while on military duty in Korea in the late 1960s and was suspected of desertion. The family could not be reunited in Japan without the father being liable to arrest and trial under American military law.

Soga, who returned to Japan alone, spoke for all five abductees when, setting foot on Japanese soil, she said:

> I am home after 24 years. It is like a dream. People's hearts, the mountains, the rivers, the valleys, all seem warm and beautiful. It is as if the skies, the earth, the trees, are gently whispering to me: 'Welcome home, you have done well,' and so in a strong voice I say, 'I am back. Thank you.'[21]

To official Japan, however, the human pain and joy seemed secondary. Nakayama Kyoko, who as special minister of state was assigned responsibility for handling the abduction matter, said, "I have from the beginning thought of this as a matter for the state. The feelings of the people themselves are of course important, but more important is the response of the country."[22]

Six months after her return to Japan, Soga poignantly asked:

> Wait, be patient, we are told, but we want actions, not just words . . . My father, mother, sister and I were one family. My husband and daughters and I were another. Who has divided these families? Who will reunite them?[23]

Her words were profoundly ambiguous. Her original family had plainly been torn apart by her North Korean abductors, but her second family, her American husband and her daughters, had been ruptured by the Japanese government's decision to renege on its agreement with Pyongyang. Two months after being thus blocked from return to her family, she was a second time prevented from return, this time by the intervention of a senior cabinet delegation that traveled to her remote island home to stop her.[24] As the autumn of her return to Japan lengthened into winter, then spring and summer, her appeal for help remained unanswered.

As the drama of these families unfolded before the nation, major television channels, newspapers, and journals catered to, and in turn cultivated, a mass market of hostility, fear, and prejudice. From 1991 to 2003, some 600 books on North Korea were published in Japanese, the overwhelming majority of them virulently hostile.[25] From the Koizumi visit to Pyongyang in September 2002, television offered almost saturation coverage on North Korea, often three or four separate programs during a single day, exposing one of an other aspect of North Korean state and society: defector stories, poverty and starvation stories, lurid and sensational accounts of life close to Kim Jong Il, stories of corruption, missiles, and nuclear threats. The memoirs of the defector, Hwang Jang Yop, published in Korean with the title *I Saw the Truth of History: Memoirs of Hwang Jang Yop*, called in Japanese *Declaration of War on Kim Jong Il: Memoirs of Hwang Jang Yop*. A second volume of his was published with the Japanese title of *Have No Fear of a Mad Dog*.[26] A *manga* (comic book) life of Kim Jong Il published in mid-2003, depicting Kim as a violent, bloodthirsty, and depraved despot, sold a half million copies in its first three months, probably more than all books *ever* published about North Korea in all other languages put together.

Glancing through the books published just in the past six months, one finds titles like *Don't be Taken in by the North Korean Terror State, A True Picture of North Korean Evil—First Scenes of the Astonishing Reality of Life in the Kim Kingdom on the Brink of Col-*

*lapse, A Complete Record of the Struggle of the Abductee Families against Kim Jong Il, Sex in North Korea—a Survival Necessity, The Devil of Our North Korean Homeland,* and *The Truth about Kim Jong Il—The Sly and Tricky General.* Weekly and monthly magazine stories poured out at a phenomenal rate, their messages almost always as uncompromising. In the uncertain political and economic climate of the early twenty-first century, Japanese readers seemed to relish stories of unmitigated "evil," especially when spiced with lots of prurient detail. Nothing seemed to sell better than details of Kim Jong Il's complicated family life, his wives, mistresses, and the *yorokobigumi,* or "happiness brigade," of young women who evidently constituted some sort of harem for him. With hundreds of such titles to choose from, the wonder is that the demand appeared not to flag.

The fierceness of Japanese hostility to North Korea, and the linked reluctance to face Japan's crimes against Korea, may stem in some measure from the fact that North Korea so closely resembles the Japan that many middle-aged Japanese remember from the 1940s and so could be seen as an affront, a kind of burlesque, second-class representation of Japan's form of divine, myth-based state. Hostility to North Korea is strongest among those conservatives and neonationalists whose prescription for their own country—imperial, patriarchal, monolithic, patriotic, anti-Western—is actually closer to the reality of North Korea than to that of any conventional, citizen-based democracy. Both countries, superficially poles apart, preserve at a deep level a mythological, imagined identity as special, unique, and superior, rather than a frame of citizenship, popular sovereignty, and equality.

In Pyongyang, Japan's breach of agreement was viewed seriously. The children could not simply be "handed over" (even against their will, as the Japanese side implied). Pyongyang had, in fact, initially suggested that the abductees take their children with them on their visit, but the offer had been declined, so the imputation of bad faith, and the suggestion that the abductees, if once returned to their Pyongyang homes, might never be allowed out again, was gratuitous and insulting. Paradoxically, it was now a spokesman for the North Korean Foreign Ministry who made the greatest effort to place the actual abductees at the center of the problem and who showed most sympathy for the human complexity:

> There is a reason why we did not send back [the abductees] permanently—if they were things we could have just sent them back, but they are people. They have lived in North Korea for over twenty years, married, had children, grown accustomed to our culture and customs, and they have come to conform to the standards and way of life of our society. Their children do not know their parents are Japanese and they have the same hatred for Japan for having caused pain and harm to the people of Korea as the other children of our country. Their parents have been working for our republic and enjoying a treatment above that of ordinary people. They have affection for people and all sorts of human connections.
>
> What would be their response if they were just suddenly told: 'You are all Japanese and therefore get out.' Whatever our intent, that would be tantamount to saying: 'You are no longer needed and therefore, go'. It would be a psychological blow to them and they would likely feel betrayed. In particular, the children do not know Japanese and are completely ignorant of the customs, habits, and order of Japanese society. Because of our consideration for such matters, things are not just able to be settled at a stroke by bundling them off now like things.[27]

Whatever the Pyongyang motive is behind such an utterance, it expressed a humanity and sympathy for the human plight buried by the nationalist sentiments in most of the Japanese statements. A concerted Japanese campaign developed, not only over the children of the Pyongyang Five but also over the daughter of the abducted badminton player, Kim Hyegyong. A barrage of Japanese efforts was launched to persuade this young girl, brought up by her North Korean father after the death of her mother when she was five years old, to leave home and "visit" her grandparents in Japan. Interviewed by Japanese television, she tearfully asked why her grandparents, having promised to visit her, now insisted that she come to see them instead. They responded with the offer of a visit to Tokyo's Disneyland. After initially wavering in their desire to visit her regardless of the consequences, her grandparents were gradually incorporated as central figures in the campaign to denounce Kim Jong Il and force his overthrow. When the teenager announced on television that her life was devoted to serving her country and her "Dear Leader," this too was taken as evidence of brainwashing. Yet by law—certainly by North Korean law—the rights of the child herself and, pending her maturity, those of her North Korean father, have priority. Japanese government statements made it likely, however, that any "visit" to Japan would be a one-way trip, as it had become for the five "returnees."

When follow-up talks on normalization were held in in Kuala Lumpur in late October, the North Korean delegates were asked to show more "sincerity" and were told that "Japan and North Korea seemed to place a different value on people's lives." In late October 2002, it was announced that compensation would be demanded from North Korea for the abductions of the 1970s and 1980s. In this there was a breathtaking insensitivity, if not hypocrisy, since Tokyo has always ruled out any compensation to the former "comfort women," slave laborers, and other victims of the colonial era, many of them abducted, and had waited patiently for decades for Pyongyang to weaken its position to the point where this would be precluded. The Japanese message to Pyongyang therefore seemed to be precisely the opposite of what its delegate proclaimed in Kuala Lumpur: Korean and Japanese lives were indeed of different value, a handful of Japanese lives weighing far more than hundreds of thousands, indeed millions, of Korean ones.

The pain of "Japan as victim" thus served to eclipse any sense of the pain caused by "Japan as aggressor." Calls for retribution were uttered from high quarters. Korean institutions in Japan were placed under guard. Death threats were reported.[28] The conservative paper, the *Yomiuri*, began to use words like *odious* in reference to North Korea, while the *Asahi* asked editorially, "Is it really necessary to establish diplomatic ties with such an unlawful nation?" An opinion survey conducted by the Cabinet Research Office in January 2003 found that 43 percent of Japanese people believed there was a danger of Japan being caught up in a war, and their fears were overwhelmingly concentrated on the Korean peninsula.[29]

Specialists declared that there was almost no possibility that North Korea would attack Japan and that the only scenario to be really alarmed about involved a preemptive American attack on North Korean bases or nuclear sites, but fear still spread.[30] Prime Minister Koizumi, responsive to the popular mood, denounced North Korea as a "disgraceful state that abducts and kills people." For Cabinet Secretary Fukuda it was "a crazy nation," and for (then) Deputy Cabinet Secretary Abe its behavior was "gangsterish."[31] Even before the revelations of September, Tokyo Governor Ishihara commented to *Newsweek* magazine that his way of solving the North Korea problem would be to declare war on it.[32] Despite his many outrageous utterances, he remains Japan's most popular politician, tipped by some as a possible future prime minister. The tragedy of the abductees continues, their rights and wishes honored in the abstract, but in practice secondary to the *amour propre* of roused mass opinion and a government swayed by a fierce anti-North Korean media mobilization.

Japan retreated from any attempt to understand the historical roots of Pyongyang's worldview, make "sincere" amends for the colonial and Cold War past, or cooperate in the process of Pyongyang's attempted opening. The government seemed committed to a belief that Pyongyang was steadily weakening to the point where it would have no alternative but to return to the negotiating table on Japanese terms, with Japan's money as an ultimately irresistible card.

One of Japan's leading authorities on North Korea, Tokyo University Emeritus Professor Wada Haruki, believes that it may now be in the throes of a power struggle, with Kim Jong Il's commitments to openness and reform, scarcely reported in the North Korean media (much less outside the country), contested by "hardliners." If Wada is right, then Kim may be in a position similar to Gorbachev's in the last days of the Soviet Union: isolated in a rigid and conservative establishment and able to advance reform only by a zigzag process. His failure to accomplish anything by his concessions of 2002 might force him to make amends by being more responsive to the hardliners.

As the brief moment of the unilateral Koizumi initiative passed, Washington applied its considerable resources to bring Tokyo back in line with its policy of encircling and squeezing Pyongyang into submission. For the Pentagon in particular, the prospect that Japan might ever begin to "walk its own walk," perhaps by diluting its Washington alliance by some kind of "Asianism," is a nightmare scenario; it remains fundamental to the Bush administration as to those before it that Japan "continue to rely on U.S. protection." Any attempt to replace the current east Asian security architecture based on bilateral U.S. alliances with Japan and South Korea by a settlement on the

Korean peninsula, especially if linked to an entente with China, would "deal a fatal blow to US political and military influence in East Asia."[33]

The Bush administration has made clear its demand for Japan to revise its peace constitution and expand its defense horizons in order to support "coalition" operations anywhere on earth as a fully fledged NATO-style partner or, as the "Armitage Report" on U.S.–Japan relations (dated October 2000 and named after the present Deputy Secretary of State Richard Armitage) put it, turn itself into the "Britain of the Far East."[34] The meaning of Japan's alliance with the United States, long seen as a trade-off of bases for global market reach, assumed a different complexion in the post–September 11 world. This was especially true in the light of the Bush administration's redefinition of America' role in its September 2002 National Security Strategy as sole global hegemon, justifying not only preemptive but preventive war and giving notice that preemptive nuclear strikes were under consideration.[35]

Some had argued that Koizumi's Pyongyang visit presaged a dramatic break with half a century of close coordination in foreign policy between Washington and Tokyo, but a year later the reverse seemed to be true—the tentative moves toward an autonomous diplomatic initiative had been squashed and Koizumi was firmly in step with his "alliance partner." Washington seemed confident that Koizumi was "our man," second only to Tony Blair in faithfulness and therefore worth a ten-hour overnight stopover at Bush's Crawford ranch in May 2003. South Korea's Roh Moo Hyun would get only half an hour a few weeks later. But there were reasons for nagging anxiety. Paradoxically, Japan is easier held in rein so long as North Korea is a threat. If relations between Japan and North Korea, or even between North and South Korea, were ever normalized, the tension would drain from them and the comprehensive incorporation of Japan within the American hegemonic project would become correspondingly more difficult to justify. In other words, if peace broke out in east Asia, the justification for the sprawling U.S. military base presence in South Korea and Japan would disappear. For Japan to normalize its relations with the continent and become the "Japan," of east Asia taking on a subordinator "comprador" role rather than as the "Britain" of the region, would be a nightmare for Washington.

The contemporary Japanese economic, political, and social crisis is often seen as rooted in the structures of dependence set in place during the postwar American occupation (and embraced for their own purposes by Japanese elites). The country's nationalism has therefore been understood as a form of distorted "neonationalism," either "comprador" or "parasitic"— in the sense of combining an exaggerated stress on the rhetoric and symbolism of the nation with an entrenched military and political subordination (to the United States).[36] In this view, Japan's problems can only begin to be solved and regional order established when it stands on its own feet and gives priority to its own national, regional, and global interests, rather than Washington's. Interestingly, a number of high-level former Japanese functionaries have begun to express this view.

Thus Taniguchi Makoto, Japan's former ambassador to the UN and former deputy secretary-general of the OECD, has called for a sweeping reconsideration of the "follow the United States" unrequited-love mindset within the Ministry of Foreign Affairs, and for the adoption of an Asia-centered, multilateral foreign policy. Takeoka Katsumi, former secretary-general of the Defense Agency, argues that there is no force in east Asia capable of invading Japan, and therefore many of the measures adopted at U.S. prodding in response to September 11, like the steady transformation of the alliance from a "defense of Japan" structure into one of regional and global military cooperation, are "sheer military lunacy." When "emergency" bills passed into law in June 2003 supported by a huge majority in the Diet, the "emergency" envisaged was clearly on the Korean peninsula. The legislation clears the way for Japanese mobilization in support of the United States in that event.[37] Constitutional reform to remove limits on Japan's right to possess and employ military force and to build nuclear armaments are back on the agenda.

Akiyama Masahiro, the former deputy chief of the Defence Agency, argues that "for Japan to become a true partner of the US, it should offer harsh advice when necessary." In his annual statement issued on August 6, 2002, the anniversary of his city's nuclear destruction, the mayor of Hiroshima stated that "the United States government has no right to force Pax Americana on the rest of us, or to unilaterally determine the fate of the world."[38]

From the private sector, Terashima Jitsuro, head of the Mitsui Global Problems Research Institute, also sees Japan's contemporary problems as rooted in its fifty years of viewing the world through a U.S. lens. Foreseeing a period of great confusion for Japan under the Bush administration foreign-policy doctrine, Terashima believes the time has come for Tokyo to respond by developing an autonomous doctrine of its own and, in the long run, putting an end to the American military presence on its soil.[39]

The gap between popular sentiment in the two countries also widens. When the U.S.–led war was launched on Iraq in 2003, few in Japan thought that country represented any threat. In fact half said the United States itself was a bad influence on global security, and 14 percent actually saw the United States as the major threat Japan faced.[40] Although the Japanese government hastens to comply with all requests from Washington, discontent and anxiety grow in the public at large at the cravenness of its submission to U.S. interests.

There are those who welcome Washington's pressures. Norota Hosei, chief of the Defense Agency, argued in March

1999 that, in certain circumstances, Japan's entitlement to self-defense forces (which it claims as an "inherent right" despite the extremely strict terms of the constitution's Article 9) includes the right of preemptive attack; the context made clear he was thinking of North Korea. His successor as minister of state for defense under Koizumi, Ishiba Shigeru, reiterated that stance in 2003, speaking of Japan being justified in making a preemptive strike on North Korean missile sites if it believed an attack on Japan was being prepared. Currently, a hundred Diet members belong to "Young Diet Members for the Establishment of a Security System for the twenty first-century."[41]

Nishimura Shingo, the Defense Agency's parliamentary vice-minister, raised the possibility in October 1999. The prominent conservative academic, Nakanishi Terumasa of Kyoto University, argues that the North Korean threat justifies Japan's development of its own nuclear weapons.[42] Surveys show high and rising public levels of fear and uncertainty. Such a sense of insecurity is only likely to intensify as North Korea's own insecurity is intensified. The more North Korea fears preemptive attack, the more likely that it will resort to preemptive attack, however suicidal, itself. Nuclear rumblings are more frequently heard in Japan.[43] In 2002 Fukuda Yasuo, the cabinet secretary, and Abe Shinzo, assistant cabinet secretary, argued that it was time to review Japan's "three nonnuclear principles" and that nuclear weapons would not contravene the Constitution. In June 2002 Ozawa Ichiro, leader of the Liberal Party, wrote that China should be careful not to push Japan, because "if its nationalism is aroused, calls for it to adopt nuclear weapons might emerge."[44] These are no more than straws in the wind, but the climate of anger, fear, and frustration sparked by the September 17 revelations makes Japan's course difficult to predict.

On that September day in 2002 as Japanese and North

Korean leaders reached the all too short-lived agreement, a radically different east Asian future was briefly glimpsed—one of reconciliation, normalization, economic cooperation between Japan and North Korea, de-nuclearization and demilitarization throughout the region, accelerated North-South cooperation (and, in the longer term, reunification), and a dismantling of the encrusted structures of North Korea's guerilla state.

# VII

# NUCLEAR CHICKEN: THE CONFRONTATION BETWEEN NORTH KOREA AND THE UNITED STATES

The confrontation between North Korea and the United States is so unequal that one is inclined to turn to the bible for an appropriate analogy, but while the United States may be a contemporary Goliath North Korea is no David, and it is certainly armed with more than a slingshot. In fact neighbors could be forgiven for thinking that in this contest Philistines are arrayed against Philistines: on one side, a tiny state pursues incomprehensible policies that seem to threaten mass destruction and on the other the global superpower threatens preemptive attack and insists on its right to dominate the earth. Before it spills over into catastrophe for the region, the mutual hostility of North Korea and the United States has to be resolved.

There are a number of fundamental misconceptions about this confrontation: that North Korea initiated it; that North Korea will stop at nothing in its determination to become a nuclear power; and that North Korea, unlike "normal" states, does not negotiate but merely bluffs, demands, or blackmails, and that it does not keep its promises. The truth is more complex, and responsibility is more widely shared.

• • •

## NUCLEAR DETERRENCE

While in Washington the North Korean nuclear threat has been a major issue for the past decade, in Pyongyang the U.S. nuclear threat has been the issue for the past fifty years. North Korea's uniqueness in the nuclear age lies first of all in the way it has faced and lived under the shadow of nuclear threat for longer than any other nation. During the Korean War it escaped nuclear annihilation by the barest of margins, and the relief that followed the signing of the Armistice in 1953 proved short-lived. Just four years later, and in obvious breach of the Armistice, the United States introduced nuclear artillery shells, mines, and missiles into Korea, and it added periodically thereafter to a nuclear stockpile kept adjacent to the Demilitarized Zone and designed to intimidate the nonnuclear North. When these nuclear weapons were finally withdrawn in 1991 that did little to diminish the threat as perceived by Pyongyang, since the United States openly continued its rehearsals for a long-range nuclear strike on North Korea.[1]

Facing the threat of nuclear attack for decades, it is not so surprising that minds in Pyongyang should have turned to the idea of developing a "deterrent" when the possibility arose. It is precisely this logic of threat and response, in the still-spreading wake of the U.S. development and use of nuclear weapons against Hiroshima and Nagasaki, that gave the world the Soviet (later Russian), British, French, Chinese, Indian, Pakistani, Israeli, and possibly other components of our global nuclear arsenal. If none of these countries can feel secure without nuclear weapons, how much more so must North Korea be so long subjected to the direct threat of nuclear attack?[2]

North Korea is rich in natural uranium, and during the decades of nuclear energy optimism the possibility of solving its energy problems by exploiting its own resources was attractive. From the late 1950s scientists were sent to learn nuclear technology at Soviet institutions, and in the 1960s a nuclear power research center, with a small experimental, light-water-type reactor from the Soviet Union, was constructed at Yongbyon, about sixty miles north of Pyongyang. In the 1970s, North Korea signed various agreements with the International Atomic Energy Agency (IAEA) and from 1980 it began construction work on a gas-graphite reactor, which was completed and began operation in 1986. It is this reactor that was and is the center of North Korea's nuclear problem, because it is from the wastes of this type of reactor that plutonium, a key material for nuclear weapons, is extracted.[3] Sometime in the late 1980s, as its graphite reactor commenced operation, North Korea seems to have made the decision to set about creating a plutonium-based weapons program.

In 1985, North Korea joined the nations which had signed the Non-Proliferation Treaty (NPT). It also began work on two other reactors, with a capacity of 50 and 200 MW respectively, and drew up plans for a substantial nuclear energy program involving an even larger complex of reactors (four reactors, each of 440 MW) to be built with Soviet cooperation. However, its own economic crisis and the political crisis leading to the collapse of the Soviet Union blocked this latter plan from fruition.

To the world, North Korea insisted that it was merely seeking a solution to its energy problems, using a naturally abundant fuel, but doubts and suspicions grew. The plant was thought to be too large for experimental purposes, there were several unexplained stoppages that might have been designed to allow removal of the rods for the extraction of plutonium. Nor was there a sign of any steps to channel electricity from Yongbyon to the rest of the country. Satellite photographs also seemed to show stages of reprocessing underway, and by 1991 both the Soviet KGB and the American CIA had come to the conclusion that a nuclear weapons program was indeed at an advanced stage. By 1993, the Americans estimated that already one or two weapons might have been produced.[4]

In 1991, however, the Soviet Union was dissolved. *Détente* was in the air, and a post–Cold War world offered hope for many outstanding problems to be resolved peacefully. North Korea sought, and the United States in due course agreed to, the removal of U.S. nuclear weapons from South Korea. In a rapidly warming atmosphere, North Korea signed the IAEA Safeguards Agreement and agreed to admit inspectors to its nuclear sites. For the first time, since a short-lived peninsula *détente* in 1972, South and North Korea reached a series of important agreements. They simultaneously entered the United Nations. They signed a Korean Peninsula Non-Nuclear Agreement, pledging not to "test, manufacture, produce, import, possess, store, deploy, or use" nuclear weapons and not to use waste processing or uranium enrichment facilities for those purposes. They also adopted a wide-ranging "Agreement on Reconciliation, Nonaggression and Exchanges and Cooperation between the South and the North."[5] North Korea also seemed to be moving toward normalization of relations with its oldest enemy, Japan. It welcomed a multiparty delegation headed by the Liberal-Democratic Party's Kanemaru Shin at the end of that year, while the party, in return, expressed formal regrets and apologized over Japan's colonial record.

However, the promise of *détente*, normalization and reconciliation, was not fulfilled. Instead on the Korean peninsula, the Cold War, liquidated elsewhere, survived and from 1992 even intensified. The United States and South Korea, under the newly elected administrations of George Bush and Roh Tae Woo, shifted from conciliation to ultimatum, demanding North Korea's satisfactory completion of the inspections before they would consider any further step. They tended to think that concessions were unnecessary because North Korea would soon collapse. For its part, North Korea seems to have made serious errors of judgment, evidently believing it could successfully accommodate the new world order by persisting with development of its own nuclear "deterrent" while simultaneously pursuing *détente* with its old enemies. The urgency of securing its defenses had been heightened by the loss of the Soviet nuclear umbrella. Its leaders were also aware that at various times South Africa, Brazil, Argentina, and Iraq among other nations, had been able to pursue their various nuclear programs without serious problem, since inspections had not hitherto been taken very seriously in the NPT regime. The assumption was made that it too could get away with careful management of the inspection process. However, such an analysis was flawed. The formula it adopted was both unstable and contradictory.[6]

The problem for North Korea was partly one of timing and partly one of technology. As no other country had faced such intense and prolonged hostility from the United States, so no other country would face such pressure to desist. As a path to security, an independent deterrent was by definition in North Korea's case fraught with high risk. Furthermore, advances in technology had made it much more difficult to successfully cover up a nuclear weapons program. Once the inspectors arrived, in May 1992, North Korea's Yongbyon site was subject to intense scrutiny, using technologies whose sophistication probably took the North Koreans by surprise.[7] After repeated altercations, when it became apparent that deception would not work and that the gains anticipated from *détente* were not going to accrue, Pyongyang in March 1993 announced its withdrawal from the NPT.

Nuclear weapons development had been seen as a means to two ends: security and the normalization of relations with the world. Without nuclear weapons North Korea was a poor and insignificant country; with them—perhaps only with them—it might command the attention of the United States and Japan. As soon as the United States insisted that there could be no negotiations until Pyongyang first gave up its programs and submitted to the IAEA inspections, the two sides found themselves locked in a game of chicken.

From 1993 through 1994 the crisis deepened steadily. The Clinton administration's Pentagon drew up Operations Plan 5027, designed to attack and destroy North Korea's nuclear facilities. It was estimated that such an attack could lead to full-scale war in which "as many as one million people would be killed, including 80,000 to 100,000 Americans, that the costs to the United States would exceed $100 billion, and that the destruction of property and interruption of business activity would cost more than $1 trillion."[8] The possible nuclear pollution of much of the peninsula, and perhaps beyond, either from the attack itself or from North Korea's targeting of nuclear plants in South Korea, creating one, two, or many Chernobyls, did not even figure in these calculations. When Seoul protested strongly and refused any part in the contemplated war, the United States was obliged to negotiate. With the reluctant agreement of then-President Clinton, ex-president Jimmy Carter undertook a mission to the DPRK in June 1994 and brokered a deal that later that year led to the Geneva "Agreed Framework."

### The Agreed Framework

Under this agreement, the withdrawl from NPT was canceled and North Korea was to freeze its graphite nuclear reactor program, including the 8,000-odd rods of plutonium-containing waste from the reactors, in return for two electricity-generating light-water reactors to be constructed by 2003 by a newly established Korean Peninsula Energy Development Organization (KEDO) and an interim annual supply of 3.3 million barrels of oil.[9] Though brokered by the United States, the financial obligations of this deal would be borne primarily by South Korea and Japan. The United States and North Korea agreed to "move towards full normalization of political and economic relations." While the United States was to provide "formal assurances to the Democratic People's Republic of Korea against the threat or use of nuclear weapons." The leading study of these events concludes that Pyongyang played its nuclear card "brilliantly, forcing one of the world's richest and most powerful nations to undertake negotiations and to make concessions to one of the least successful."[10] The possibility of war had, for the time being, passed. Kim Il Sung proved surprisingly open to negotiation when Carter actually sat down with him. It seemed that not only a deal for the short-term crisis but for the longer term, too, might be possible.

The North Korean energy crisis was by this stage acute. With the collapse of the Soviet Union and the embrace of market principles in Russia and in China, oil had to be imported on "commercial" rather than the accustomed "friendly" terms. Since its economy was collapsing, Pyongyang was unable to pay for the quantities it needed, and as the oil flow dried up the heavily energy-dependent agriculture sector collapsed. Nuclear energy did not make a great deal of economic sense, although the rush to nuclear power in many other countries at the time, including France and Japan, made that less than obvious. At least, the light-water reactor was a far more sophisticated and attractive option than the existing graphite system. North Korea had long preferred light-water technology but had been deterred by the cost (around $1 billion per reactor) and the fact that virtually all the key components were beyond its technological capability. In his already classic account, journalist Don Oberdorfer explains, "If it were working well, Yongbyon's only operating reactor, rated at 5 megawatts (5 million watts) would produce only enough electricity to power perhaps five large American office buildings; but two standard LWRs would produce 2,000 megawatts—nearly enough electricity to power the Washington metropolitan area."[11] In the showdown of 1994, the fact of the technology being "advanced" and expensive made the light-water reactor an attractive face-saving solution for North Korea, a satisfactorily compensation for agreeing to mothball the inefficient graphite works and desist from whatever it had been doing to produce nuclear weapons. It would also go some way toward solving the problem of its inability to purchase oil.

For Pyongyang, the Agreed Framework was not a unilateral promise to give up its nuclear ambitions in return for the construction of two reactors but a complex web of commitments. The provision that the two sides would move toward full normalization of political and economic relations and that the United States would provide formal assurances to the DPRK against the use of nuclear weapons were crucial. However, the Clinton administration, confronted by a Republican-dominated Congress that resolutely opposed any "deal" with North Korea, preferred to think that the Pyongyang regime would, following the East European example, collapse of its own contradictions, long before any nuclear technology might have to be transferred to it, and it was agonizingly slow and reluctant about its normalization commitment.

On August 16, 1998, in the fifth year of the Agreed Framework, when construction work on the promised reactors had still not begun, Washington received a rude awakening. North Korea launched its *Kwangmyongsong* satellite. Though failing to orbit, it soared dramatically across Japanese skies before splashing down in the North Pacific. Realization that Pyongyang was close to developing an intercontinental ballistic missile galvanized Washington. William Perry, secretary of defense in the Clinton administration between 1994 and 1997, was appointed special envoy with authority to negotiate and advise on North Korea policy. After an intensive, eight-month study

and a visit to Pyongyang, his report cleared Pyongyang of suspicions over alleged secret nuclear developments, confirmed
that it had abided by the freeze, and recommended a step-by-
step process toward "comprehensive normalization of relations
and the establishment of a permanent peace."[12]

Visits were then exchanged between Jo Myong Rok, vice-
marshal of the North Korean People's Army and first vice-
president of the National Defense Commission, Kim Jong Il's
right-hand man, and U.S. Secretary of State Madeleine Albright.
Marshall Jo, in the full military uniform of the Democratic
People's Republic, was received at a cordial meeting in Washington by President Clinton. A joint U.S.–North Korea communiqué reaffirmed the 1994 agreement and expressed
renewed commitment to a fundamental improvement in relations and an end to the Korean War. At this crucial juncture, on
the brink of a comprehensive settlement between the two countries, time—or presidential courage—ran out. The Clinton
administration came to an end without further progress.[13]
Never had the two countries been closer to settlement, yet
within months that momentum was lost.

### BACK TO SQUARE ONE

Under George W. Bush's administration, the Agreed Framework
was seen as Clinton appeasement, or at best nothing more than a
one-sided North Korean commitment to abandon its nuclear
program. After September 11, 2001, the U.S. attitude hardened
even further. It mattered little that Pyongyang seemed to be trying
to associate itself with the mood of the international community
by signing outstanding international conventions on terrorism
and declaring its opposition to terrorism in the UN General
Assembly, or that the State Department as of 2001 could find no
North Korean connection with global terror other than the continued hosting of the aging Japanese perpetrators of a 1970
hijacking,[14] or that Secretary of State Colin Powell believed

Pyongyang to be continuing to "comply with the [missile flight-test] moratorium they placed upon themselves and staying within the KEDO agreement [the Agreed Framework]."[15] Despite all of this, the United States still named North Korea, along with a number of other nonnuclear countries, as a potential nuclear target in its Nuclear Posture Statement submitted to Congress in December 2001, and then, in January 2002, the president called North Korea part of an "axis of evil." Its inclusion in that "axis" in the president's State of the Union speech, as ex-White House speechwriter David Frum's account makes clear, was almost accidental, springing from a desire to have one non-Islamic country lined up in the rogue shooting gallery, rather than any sense that North Korea had suddenly become a threat. But to Pyongyang it sounded like a death sentence.[16]

Whatever North Korea may or may not be guilty of in terms of breaching its international commitments, the fact is that the initial and crucial breaches were American ones. The introduction of nuclear weapons to the Korean peninsula in the first place, the refusal to take seriously its obligations under the Non Proliferation Treaty to "negotiate in good faith to achieve a precise result—nuclear disarmament in all its aspects" and the inclusion of North Korea on the nuclear target list were all breaches of the Non Proliferation Treaty. The United States was also in breach of the Agreed Framework by its dilatoriness at the planned light-water reactor site—the "2003" pledge was never taken seriously—where construction only began in 2002 when a few large holes were dug in the ground and foundations laid, by its refusal to countenance any steps toward the promised normalization of relations, and by issuing the threatening labels of "rogue state" and "axis of evil." Pyongyang interpreted this sequence of events as indicative of aggressive American intent.

Even if North Korea had gone about secretly producing its own nuclear deterrent, whether it was actually in breach of international law or treaty was unclear. The International Court of Justice said in 1996 that it "cannot reach a definitive conclusion as to the legality or illegality of the use of nuclear weapons by a state in an extreme circumstance of self-defense, in which its very survival would be at stake."[17] The Agreed Framework forbade work on the Yongbyon reactor and the reprocessing of the spent fuel rods, and Pyongyang complied. The purchase of uranium enrichment centrifuge devices from Pakistan was, however, a distinct breach of the South-North Non-Nuclear Peninsula agreement.

From North Korea's perspective, the world is full of nuclear hypocrisy. Nonnuclear countries are forced to bow to the great powers that possess the bomb. While entry into the "nuclear club" earns the respect of current club members, outsiders who attempt to join it are threatened with annihilation. Washington demands that North Korea disavow any nuclear plans (and substantially cut back on its conventional forces), but the United States retains an actively deployed arsenal of 7,650 nuclear warheads (most of them "strategic" and far more powerful than the one used at Hiroshima) with a further 3,600 in reserve or awaiting dismantling.[18] The U.S. has withdrawn from the Comprehensive Nuclear Test-Ban Treaty, the Anti-Ballistic Missile Treaty, the Biological Weapons Convention, the International Criminal Court, and the Kyoto Convention on Global Warming. It signals its intent to pursue nuclear hegemony including the domination of space; deploys as "conventional weapons" newly developed weapons of terror and mass destruction including cluster bombs, "daisy cutters," and depleted uranium-tipped shells; and is working to develop a new generation of nuclear "bunker buster" bombs and a space-based weapons system, enabling it to target anyplace on earth. It proclaims its right to assassinate or launch preemptive war against its enemies and refuses to recognize the jurisdiction of any international court to try its actions or those of its citizens.

For three decades it has ignored its obligations under Article 6 of the 1968 Non-Proliferation Treaty to "pursue negotiations in good faith . . . to nuclear disarmament" (and is therefore in "material breach" of the treaty), while insisting that others honor it strictly. None of this, however, in the eyes if the U.S. is "roguish" or "evil." Pyongyang sees the United States consistently placing itself above the law, reserving to itself the right to employ violence, virtually without restriction, in pursuit of its global interests, while labeling "terroristic" those who oppose it.

U.S.–North Korea relations under George W. Bush's presidency have so far been marked by three dramatic and controversial encounters, in Pyongyang in October 2002, in Beijing in April of that year and then again in Beijing in September 2003.

### PYONGYANG, OCTOBER 2002

On October 3, 2002, just weeks after Japanese Prime Minister Koizumi's visit to Pyongyang, a special presidential envoy, Deputy Secretary of State James Kelly, was dispatched to North Korea. His visit occurred in the context of rapidly improving North Korean relations with both South Korea and Japan and had the effect of quickly reversing that momentum.

Kelly did not go to negotiate but to confront North Korea with proof of its bad behavior. He presented evidence of a covert uranium-enrichment program and called on North Korea to "dramatically alter its behavior across a range of issues, including its WMD programs, development and export of ballistic missiles, threats to its neighbors, support for terrorism, and the deplorable treatment of the North Korean people."[19] Where the first presidential envoy to Pyongyang, William Perry, had brought the olive branch of *détente* from Clinton, Kelly brought this ultimatum from Bush. He evidently expected his hosts to deny the charges, but to his surprise First Vice-Minister Kang Song Ju— according to Kelly anyway—admitted to a uranium-enriching program and possession of "other weapons" that were "even more powerful."

The account given by the American side of what was said at these meetings did more than anything else to build the sense of an imminent North Korean "threat" around the world. However, the Washington story deserves a scrutiny no less skeptical and careful than has, belatedly, been given to the case for war against Iraq.[20]

The allegations of uranium enrichment were quite separate from the previous allegations concerning the processing of plutonium from spent fuel rods in the Yongbyon reactor. Where plutonium is the material for nuclear weapons of the Nagasaki type, enriched uranium is the material for the more primitive Hiroshima-type weapon. Washington had evidently received intelligence to the effect that Pakistan, having succeeded in producing its own plutonium-based weapon, had transferred unwanted gas centrifuges for uranium enrichment to North Korea, probably in 1999. Since North Korea too was already at an advanced state in plutonium technology, one can only assume that it was covering its bets by taking delivery of the centrifuges. It has subsequently insisted that it has no enrichment program (without denying that it actually possesses the centrifuges). The gas centrifuges cannot be employed without considerable quantities of aluminum compound, which intelligence sources appear to have concluded that Pyongyang had not been able to acquire. Its denial of operation was therefore plausible.[21] To the UN, North Korea subsequently admitted that it had indeed purchased, but not operated, uranium-enrichment devices.[22]

Newspapers around the world, however, headlined Pyongyang's "admission" that it had "an active nuclear weapons program," and the reports of the admission undoubtedly undermined Pyongyang's credibility. On October 16, 2002, White House spokesman Sean McCormack announced that Pyongyang was in "material breach" of its agreement with the United States and Washington promptly insisted that its northeast Asian allies cooperate in applying political and economic pressure to enforce compliance. Kenneth Quinones, one of the most experienced American negotiators with North Korea, remarked that it "strengthened the influence of Washington's 'hardliners' who favor pressuring Pyongyang, even to the point of war."[23] The "admissions" were in turn used as an excuse to suspend what little work was being done on the light-water reactor construction site and on November 14, 2002, under heavy U.S. pressure the executive board of KEDO announced that it was suspending desperately needed fuel-oil deliveries, just as winter was beginning.[24]

It is far from clear, however, what exactly Kang admitted. He was Pyongyang's most experienced negotiator and its signatory on the 1994 agreement. Confronted, possibly, with copies of receipts or other documentary evidence of a deal with Pakistan, he may have felt obliged to admit to the possession of the centrifuge technology, but that in itself did not necessarily constitute an "active nuclear weapons program." Why would Kang go out of his way to challenge the United States by insisting that North Korea had this *and more?* An official statement from the Korean Central News Agency quickly declared that, faced with an "extremely high-handed and arrogant" Kelly, who seemed uninterested in dialogue and merely "keen to . . . destroy the Korean-style socialist system," the DPRK made very clear "that the DPRK was *entitled to possess* [italics added] not only nuclear weapons but any type of weapon more powerful than that, so as to defend its sovereignty and right to existence from the ever-growing nuclear threat by the US."[25] A North Korean foreign ministry official added, "I clearly say that we denied from the start their allegations of a nuclear weapons program using enriched uranium."[26] Weeks after the Beijing talks, when the *Washington Post*'s Don Oberdorfer visited Pyongyang for "more than nine hours of talks" with many of the same officials Kelly had met, they vehemently denied Kelly's widely publicized account. Kang Sok Ju insisted that the words of the Foreign Ministry statement repeated exactly what he had said to Kelly.[27] Oberdorfer also reported his strong impression that the door was still "wide open for a peaceful resolution"[28] (though official Washington denied this).

However, the 1994 Agreed Framework froze only the plutonium-related Yongbyon reactor works and the rods of waste plutonium. It is true that Pyongyang also accepted an obligation to allow inspections by the International Atomic Energy Agency, but only when "a significant portion" of the [KEDO] reactors were complete and before "key nuclear components" were delivered. Since the KEDO reactor works had fallen far behind schedule, Pyongyang was in breach of no obligation to the IAEA at the time of the Kelly visit.

In Seoul, many thought that Washington might have "misunderstood," perhaps even deliberately distorted, what had been said in Pyongyang.[29] One theory was that the reference to something "even more powerful" than nuclear weapons might have been a rhetorical allusion to the power of the "unity of the Workers Party and people," rather than a sinister chemical or biological doomsday project as U.S. statements assumed. Kim Dae Jung's senior presidential advisor also questioned the timing of the U.S. revelation, coinciding as it did with the Koizumi visit, the brief Pyongyang-Tokyo thaw, and a rapidly growing momentum in North-South economic cooperation.[30] Could it be, he inquired, that Washington did not want peace and reconciliation to break out between the two Koreas and Japan?

The maximum North Korean offense at this point was the purchase of the centrifuges. The plutonium reactor and reprocessing works remained frozen. However, smarting at the Kelly insults and faced with the suspension of the reactor construction works and the heavy oil shipments, Pyongyang in December discon-nected the IAEA's monitoring cameras, removed the seals and sent home the inspectors from its mothballed graphite plant. On January 9, 2002, it announced that it was withdrawing from the Nuclear Non-Proliferation Treaty and would soon restart its Yongbyon reactors. This, it said, was necessary because the inter-national agreements entered into at Geneva could no longer be relied upon and consequently North Korea would have to act to solve its acute energy problem in its own way. Though it insisted that "at present" the reactors were merely being started up for "energy purposes," neighboring states were understandably nervous at the prospect of unregulated plutonium production, while the enrichment technology (whose possession it admitted) has no known use other than for the production of Hiroshima-type weapons. Washington ratcheted up its cam-paign against North Korea as an "outlaw" regime, defying the world and threatening regional and global order. Pyongyang had apparently concluded that the only way to capture U.S. attention and move forward on the range of issues that concerned it was to reopen the reactor program. Subsequent events suggest they may have been right.

### DEADLOCK, OCTOBER 2002–APRIL 2003

In January 2003, the Bush administration began to talk about a bold "new proposal." Pyongyang would still be required to abandon all nuclear ambitions and accept strict and intrusive inspections, but, provided it did so, assistance could be given with thermal power generation replacing the light-water reactors, the provision of food aid, and a guarantee of some undefined sort against U.S. attack.[31] However, the offer was predicated on a North Korean climb-down, which was made unlikely by the hostile rhet-oric that accompanied it. With an Iraq war looming, Secretary of Defense Donald Rumsfeld reiterated America's readiness to fight, and win, wars on "two fronts"—meaning that it was potentially willing to take on war on Korea as well as Iraq and confident "of winning decisively in one and swiftly defeating the enemy in the case of the other."[32] North Korea was accused again of being a "terrorist regime" with "one or two nuclear weapons already in possession and sufficient material to construct six to eight more, and missile capacity to reach the continental United States."[33] In his State of the Union address for 2003, President Bush denounced Pyongyang as "an oppressive regime [that] rules a people living in fear and starvation," whose "blackmail" would not be tolerated.[34] Long-range bombers and an aircraft carrier were alerted for deployment to the region. Pyongyang in due course responded, not to the "new proposal" but to the threats, with its own threat of possible missile or weapon tests or even a preemptive counterstrike, involving "unlimited use of means [sic]."[35]

On February 13, Mohammad El Baradei, the International Atomic Energy Agency's director-general, declared North Korea to be "in chronic non-compliance with its safeguards agreement since 1993" and by a unanimous vote the IAEA referred the matter to the UN Security Council.[36] China and Russia blocked any move in the Security Council,[37] fearing it would most likely lead to sanctions, and sanctions, according to Pyongyang, would be tantamount to "a declaration of war."[38] In any case, Pyongyang's withdrawal from the IAEA raised the question of how a nonmember could be bound by its rules.

As the crisis evolved, the North Korean regime repeatedly declared its readiness, as it had at the Pyongyang meeting with Koizumi, to enter into formal, internationally binding commitments—or strictly speaking to honor those it had already entered—if only the United States would withdraw the threats to its existence and move to normalize relations with it. This was more or less what it was promised in 1994.

If the US legally commits itself to non-aggression against the DPRK through the non-aggression pact, the DPRK will be able to rid the US of its security concerns. Although the DPRK has left the NPT, its nuclear activity at present is limited to the peaceful purpose of power generation. If the US gives up its hostile policy toward the DPRK and refrains from posing a nuclear threat to it, it may prove that it does not manufacture nuclear weapons through a special verification between the DPRK and the US.[39]

This, for Secretary of State Colin Powell, was "intimidation" or "bad behavior" to which the United States would not submit. The words *blackmail* and *intimidation* tripped regularly off the tongues of U.S. officials. Secretary Rumsfeld likewise ruled out negotiations when he said, in April 2003, that there was "no price that we would be willing to pay, that they would be willing to accept, to stop engaging in what they are doing with respect to nuclear weapons."[40]

Pyongyang was, of course, hardly sweetness and light. It issued regular bloodcurdling, public pronouncements about its "tremendous military deterrent,"[41] and predictions that "a war between North Korea and the United States would end with the delightful victory of North Korea, an emerging military power, in 100 hours . . . [the United States would be] enveloped in flames" and the "arrogant empire of a devil" would breathe its last.[42] Pyongyang's occasional protestations in this vein were shrill, but its fundamental negotiating position remained remarkably consistent.

When the Bush Administration from time to time claimed that it was ready for talks with North Korea "any time, any place, without preconditions," it meant talks *to* North Korea "about how it would fulfill its obligations to the international community," readmit the inspectors, and cut back on conventional weapons, not negotiations *with* North Korea.[43] South Korean proposals early in 2003 for resolving the deadlock were dismissed with the statement that Washington did not intend to "enter" negotiations with North Korea.[44] The Bush administration seemed not to understand, wrote Desaix Anderson, a former senior U.S. diplomat and the former executive director of KEDO, that "diplomacy essentially means negotiations between two parties with different goals. It is not just coercion. . . . The Administration should overcome its puerile distaste for dealing with Kim Jong Il."[45]

### BEIJING, APRIL 2003

While maintaining its stance of refusal to "negotiate" with North Korea until all its demands were met, the United States made a tactical shift (to which Pyongyang reluctantly and under considerable pressure agreed). The forum for exchanges was shifted from the bilateral to the multilateral. The American intention was to construct a united front of neighboring countries to bring concentrated pressure to bear on North Korea. Because of China's role as North Korea's lifeline—supplier of between 50 and 80 percent of its oil and more than half of its food imports—it was assigned a key role.[46] In April 2003 a "three-sided" conference was convened in Beijing. China was either a full participant in the talks, in Washington's view, or it was the neutral host and facilitator, according to Pyongyang.

Pyongyang presented to Kelly a detailed, three-stage "roadmap" for possible resolution of the problems, offering to abandon its nuclear and missile programs and in exchange calling for a U.S. nonaggression guarantee (not necessarily in the form of a treaty, according to some accounts)[47] and the opening of diplomatic relations, economic aid, and compensation for the delay in construction of the light-water reactors and their early completion.[48] Again, the Kelly team showed no interest. Rather than negotiate, it insisted on Pyongyang's unconditional and unilateral dismantling of its nuclear program in a verifiable manner before any discussion of other matters even began. The Pyongyang proposals were dismissed as, in George Bush's terms, "back to the old blackmail game."[49] The U.S. ambassador in Tokyo, Howard Baker, described them as "their usual mix of ambiguous statements, harsh rhetoric, and what I call serial provocations," in the face of which the United States would remain "calm and patient."[50]

The American side then circulated a story, immediately given sensational publicity around the world, to the effect that Ri Gun, the chief North Korean delegate, had taken Kelly aside during a tea break and confessed to having nuclear weapons, adding, "[W]e can't dismantle them. It's up to you whether we do a physical demonstration or transfer of them." In some versions of this tale, he explicitly threatened to sell nuclear weapons to terrorists.[51] There has been no corroboration of this bizarre exchange. Chinese foreign ministry officials denied any knowledge of it, and other witnesses gave quite different versions, according to which Ri had said nothing about nuclear possession but merely that North Korea might react to further U.S. provocation by "taking physical measures."[52] Japanese media sources saw this as a deliberate leak contrived by Washington hard-liners to convey the impression that negotiations with North Korea were impossible.[53] In other words, in a pattern closely resembling that of the October talks, a North Korean proposal for comprehensive settlement, which seemed to offer plausible grounds for actual negotiation, was torpedoed by an alleged threat issued in private and denied by those who are supposed to have made it.

Despite an intensive concentration on North Korea by a significant part of the world's intelligence agencies, there was still in 2003 uncertainty about what that country might or might not have developed by way of nuclear weapons. The CIA in January 2003 revised its long-established stance that North Korea had "one or two" nuclear weapons to say only that it had "enough plutonium for at least one, possibly two."[54] In other words, the intelligence repeatedly cited over the preceding decade had been incorrect. South Korea, through its president, reiterated its belief, too, that "there is no compelling proof" North Korea has such weapons.[55] Russian specialists consistently denied that North Korea had the military and economic capacity to produce nuclear weapons. On the other hand, in July, U.S. intelligence reported rapid advances in North Korea, "combining their two most advanced weapons projects—nuclear technology and missile technology," that could, it was claimed, result in successful miniaturization of a nuclear weapon within a year.[56]

As Russia and South Korea suggested, however, it was no less plausible that North Korea's nuclear program was smoke and mirrors rather than substance. Believing that the United States respected and feared only nuclear weapons and, faced with repeated accusations of possessing them, it might have decided to bluff the Americans and claim to "possess" them even when it did not. In that case it was a dangerous game. As the two governments glared at each other and rattled their sabers, it became more difficult for either side to back down. The longer the stalemate continued, the more likely it became that the options would indeed be reduced to two: war or a nuclear-armed North Korea.

In late May–early June, a delegation of six congressmen headed by Republican Kurt Weldon went to Pyongyang to discuss various ways in which the concerns of both sides might be met. On his return, Weldon reported Pyongyang's by-now familiar plea: above all it wanted a nonaggression agreement.[57] Based on their talks, Weldon's team proposed an initial one-year nonaggression pact followed by official and verifiable renunciation of Pyongyang's nuclear weapons and research program, diplomatic recognition, and a substantial aid package involving the United States, South Korea, Japan, Russia, and China. Their proposal met a "positive response" in Pyongyang, but drew only cold water in Washington.[58]

Weldon also brought back to Washington the news that

North Korea said it had "completed" reprocessing the 8,000-odd plutonium rods held in storage since 1994.[59] This was certainly not true, since South Korean intelligence estimated in October that the process was still only about one-third complete.[60] Pyongyang was plainly trying to bluff Washington into believing that its nuclear program was more advanced than it actually was. The escalating psychological warfare between the two sides made it increasingly difficult to assess claims on either side.

When Pyongyang's Korea Central News Agency for the first time made reference to the plan to construct a nuclear deterrent, was that a statement of fact or a bluff? Naturally, this "deterrent" would not be "aimed to threaten or blackmail" anyone but would be purely defensive, with the additional purpose of reducing expenditure on conventional armaments.[61] William Perry evidently took this statement very seriously, referring to the "nightmare scenario" that by the end of 2003 Pyongyang would indeed have six to eight nuclear weapons and the capacity to continue producing them at five to ten per year, resulting in an arsenal of forty-five by the end of the decade.[62] He concluded that much of the responsibility attached to the president: "I think he has come to the conclusion that Kim Jong Il is evil and loathsome and it is immoral to negotiate with him."[63]

As the standoff continued and as a "surgical" bombing strike was ruled out, at least for the time being, U.S. efforts to destabilize North Korea were also actively pursued. The American door has been opened encouragingly to a small number of refugees from the North,[64] and the process of "discreetly but actively encouraging senior level defections . . . by offering financial support and amnesty" seems to have been adopted.[65] Previous South Korean efforts to destabilize the regime by bribery backfired when in 1997 a group of officials in touch with the South was purged and executed,[66] but reports early in

2003 spoke of senior officials and scientists being successfully extracted from the country, including "the father of North Korea's nuclear program, Kyong Won-ha."[67] It is also possible that intelligence information is being manipulated to promote destabilization. The leak of contested and unconfirmed intelligence like the reports on the Kelly missions are examples. Reports of the development of small nuclear weapons capable of being attached to existing ballistic missiles, or the existence of a second, hitherto unknown secret site for nuclear weapons production, may be proven true, or they may prove to be part of such a campaign.[68] Coming so soon after similar reports were used to justify the war on Iraq, suspicion is inevitable. A more extreme form of destabilization, involving deliberate provocation such as the conducting of maneuvers designed to "drain North Korea's limited resources, strain its military, and perhaps sow enough confusion that North Korean generals might turn against the country's leader," together with plans to disrupt financial networks and sow disinformation, was said to be under consideration.[69]

Parallel with such covert destabilization programs, the Bush administration launched an intense diplomatic effort to achieve a united front among neighboring states to contain squeeze, and ultimately topple the Kim regime. A cutoff of fuel oil supplies, an intensification of spy flights, a mobilization of bombers, and a stepping up of war preparations (including the selling of new weapons systems to South Korea) steadily increased the pressure. A "Proliferation Security Initiative" conference was held in Australia in early July 2003, to try to coordinate the carrying out of an international agreement and intercept on the high seas ships of North Korea (or other countries) suspected of carrying nuclear or missile-related cargo.[70] North Korean cargo and fishing boats moving in and out of Japanese ports were already being subjected to heavy supervision, and North Korea now knows that its ships might even be forcibly boarded on the high seas.[71] Measures to constrain financial transfers to the North (especially from the sizeable Korean population in Japan) are under consideration. South Korea is being pressed hard to put on hold the various South-North economic cooperation projects, including the railway.

As the US military victory in Iraq turned sour, a split in the administration in Washington over how to deal with North Korea became obvious. Neoconservative ideologues in—and around—the department of defense and Vice President Dick Cheney's office, intent on championing the cause of "good" against "evil" and therefore on "regime change" in Pyongyang, confronted more pragmatic elements in the state department who sought the limited goal of blocking any nuclear or missile threat from North Korea and believed it possible to accomplish that by negotiation. The well-informed *New Yorker* reporter Seymour Hersh quoted an administration insider on Kim Jong Il during the run-up to the war in Iraq: "Bush and Cheney want that guy's head on a platter. Don't be distracted by all this talk about negotiations. There will be negotiations, but they have a plan, and they are going to get this guy after Iraq. He's their version of Hitler."[72] By hook or by crook—that is to say, by force if necessary but by other means if possible—neoconservative elements of the Bush administration seemed determined to topple Kim. Under-Secretary for Arms Control and National Security John Bolton spoke of North Korea as "a hellish nightmare" whose days of blackmail were over.[73]

Epitomizing the softer line, analysts at the Brookings Institution, a major Washington think tank that could hardly be accused of having sympathy for Pyongyang, wrote:

North Korea may have had one or two nuclear weapons for a decade without going on the offensive. Indeed, on the whole, its external behavior has improved substantially in recent years. Its support for terrorism is virtually non-existent, according to U.S. government sources; its missile testing moratorium continues, and its arms exports have declined substantially; it is coming clean on its history of kidnapping Japanese citizens decades ago. It is also engaging with South Korea, Japan, the United States, and the outside world in general, albeit fitfully and slowly. Certainly it is not attacking the United States or its allies.[74]

As the fight within Washington raged, the tensions beyond it, among the members of the united front it was trying to put together, became apparent. China, Russia, and South Korea insisted on the need to address North Korea's security concerns. Japan, knowing all too well from its own experience what a desperate, isolated, leader-worshipping and highly militarized regime will do if threatened by a blockade and the cutoff of vital resources, urged the United States to reconsider its hard line refusal to negotiate.[75] The *Asahi* reported in June, "even though the public is not being told, it is a fact that Tokyo is seizing every opportunity to persuade Washington against engineering a regime change in North Korea."[76] When the Japanese foreign ministry of its own accord drew up a package of incentives to offer to Pyongyang (security assurances and a promise of supply of a heavy oil) the Secretary of State Colin Powell ruled it out of order.[77] South Korea persists with its Sunshine policies of cooperation.

### BEIJING, AUGUST 2003
Through China's good offices, a second round of Beijing talks, this time six-sided, involving Russia, Japan, South Korea, the United States, China, and North Korea, was conducted in Beijing over three days at the end of August 2003.[78] The proceedings were supposed to be secret but, to everyone's surprise, it

was Pyongyang's Korean Central News Agency that, on the day after the Conference ended, published a substantial and apparently accurate account at least of the initial position statements of the delegations.[79] It is highly likely that this unexpected action stemmed from the realization that it had suffered from its failure to counter the American version of the course of the previous Pyongyang and Beijing meetings.

The opening and longest, statement to the Conference was by James Kelly, who reiterated the United States' readiness to talk to (but not negotiate with) North Korea about the elimination, "in a complete, verifiable and irreversible manner," of its nuclear program and then about "a series of issues, including missiles, conventional weapons, counterfeiting and drug smuggling, terrorism, human rights and abduction" problems. Only when such matters were resolved would it be possible to move on to discuss other matters. Pyongyang's central demand, a nonaggression treaty, he dismissed as "neither appropriate nor necessary." This uncompromising opening speech suggested there had been no change in the Bush administration's position. It might have been calculated to provoke Kim Yong-il, North Korea's vice-minister of foreign affairs, and its chief delegate, just as Kelly had provoked his opposite number in Pyongyang in October. In his own opening speech, however, Kim used prose unusually shorn of most of North Korea's customary extravagant and rhetorical language to present his country's "bold proposals" for the first time on a major diplomatic stage:

> The denuclearization of the Korean Peninsula is the general goal of the DPRK. It is not our goal to have nuclear weapons. The denuclearization of the Korean Peninsula was our initiative and it is our consistent stand and the desire of all Koreans to realize it. The US is, however, standing in its way. . . .

The Bush administration openly disclosed its attempt to use nuclear weapons after listing the DPRK as part of 'an axis of evil' and a target of a 'pre-emptive nuclear attack.' This prompted us to judge that the Bush administration is going to stifle our system by force and decide to build a strong deterrent force to cope with it. Hence, we determined to possess that force. Our deterrent force is not aimed to attack somebody without any proper reason. It is a means for self-defense to protect our sovereignty.

We can dismantle our nuclear program if the US makes a switch over in its hostile policy towards us and does not pose any threat to us. The benchmark for our judgment that the US no longer antagonizes us will be provided only when a non-aggression treaty is concluded between the DPRK and the US, diplomatic relations opened between them and the US does not obstruct our economic dealing with other countries.

The non-aggression treaty called for by us is by no means to demand 'security assurances,' but to have a non-aggression treaty with legal biding force whereby both signatories commit themselves to non-aggression. The US cannot shirk its responsibility for having suspended the implementation of the agreed framework. We have fully fulfilled our commitment to freeze our nuclear facility since the adoption of the agreed framework.

Kelly who came to the DPRK as a special envoy of president Bush in October 2002, failing to present any specific 'evidence,' groundlessly pulled us up, using coercive words and behaving rudely, ignoring the oriental custom. He claimed that we have secretly pushed forward an enriched uranium program in breach of the agreed framework.

In this regard we made it clear that we have no secret nuclear program but we are entitled to have weapons more powerful than those based on enriched uranium. We have powerful weapons, including single-hearted unity. After Kelly's Pyongyang visit, the US misled the public opinion, saying that we admitted to the secret nuclear program and unilaterally stopped the supply of heavy fuel oil from November 2002. The DPRK–US agreed framework concluded in October 1994 was thus nullified due to the US unilateral refusal to fulfill its commitments.

The DPRK has abided by the principle that the measures for settling the nuclear issue between the DPRK and the US should be implemented by simultaneous actions. These actions provide a realistic way of realizing the denuclearization of the Korean Peninsula.

The parties could come to no agreement, even on a final communiqué, so on the third and final day the head of the host delegation, Chinese Vice Foreign Minister Wang Yi, issued a six-point "consensus statement." He declared that the parties had agreed to continue talking and not take any action prejudicial to the goal of a nuclear-free Korean peninsula, that they would take steps to address North Korea's security concerns, and that they would seek a just and realistic solution by "parallel and synchronous steps" to bridge the gap between the parties.[80]

This Conference statement overrode American objections to a phased path to settlement, something hitherto rejected as "submission to blackmail," and adopted the formula "parallel and synchronous," thereby dismissing the long-held U.S. insistence that Pyongyang must first disarm itself and that North Korean security guarantees were "neither appropriate nor necessary" (as Kelly put it). What this means is that the six-sided forum, conceived in Washington as an instrument to bring multiple and inescapable pressure to bear on Pyongyang was turned into something quite different: an instrument to pressure Washington into fundamental policy change. The center for negotiations also shifted subtly, away from Washington. Beijing's role became crucial, and the importance of an emerging Beijing–Seoul–Moscow nexus grew. Far from the United States orchestrating the proceedings, it suffered rebuke when they ended. Asked what the biggest obstacle had been, Wang Yi replied, "The American policy towards DPRK—this is the main problem we are facing."[81]

The only two parties to the Conference who shared a common language were the Koreans, and it was notable that, when the North Korean delegation had difficulty understanding the nuances of the American position, they held a private meeting with their Southern colleagues to clarify them. Other positive reports told of concerted Russian, South Korean, and various American (nonadministration) moves to address North Korea's energy and communications problems by constructing a pipeline to bring natural gas from Sakhalin Island across the Korean peninsula, a vast project that could only be conceived and carried forward in an atmosphere of regional peace and cooperation;[82] Russian and South Korean interest in restoring the rail link across North Korea was well known. Between northern and southern Korean economic delegations, intensive discussions on a whole range of economic cooperation matters continued.

## DEAL OR SHOWDOWN?
The Kim Jong Il regime is indefensible, but violent intervention to change it is more likely to lead to the sort of chaos that is engulfing Iraq and Afghanistan than to a resolution of problems that, in the last resort, only the Korean people, North and South, can solve. The necessary condition for them to do this is the "normalization" of the Korean peninsula, with problems ignored for far too long finally addressed: the lack of any peace treaty to settle the Korean War, the absence of diplomatic relations between North Korea and the two powers that above all

hold the key to North Korea's and the region's furture, the United States and Japan, and, above all, the resolution of the militarized tension that has blighted the lives of North Korea's people for half a century and created the conditions within which Kim Jong Il's dictatorship could sustain itself.

During the year that followed James Kelly's Pyongyang visit, the facilities frozen for ten years were restarted, while, at least, some of the plutonium rods were removed from the cooling ponds and the plutonium extracted, presumably for processing into weapons. Programs probably dormant since the early 1990s may have been reactivated as a result of the failure of diplomacy since George W. Bush's administration took over in Washington.[83]

Paradoxically, almost nobody accuses North Korea of aggressive intent. Its neighbors—with the qualified exception of Japan—tend to fear the United States more than North Korea. Most outside Washington would agree with Seoul's Ministry of Unification: "[T]heir true aim is not to continue the nuclear-development program, but to seek a breakthrough in relations with the United States."[84] Their behavior is better seen, according to one seasoned observer, not as "irrational brinkmanship" but as "premeditated coercive diplomacy."[85] The failure of attempts at diplomatic settlement, and the conviction that Iraq was attacked precisely because it did *not* have weapons of mass destruction, might well have led Pyongyang to believe that only its possession (or, equally effective, the ability to persuade the enemy of such possession) can deter the United States from attack. Pyongyang feels that it has been at the receiving end of America's, in historian Bruce Cumming's phrase,[86] "exterminist hatred" for fifty years since fighting U.S.-led forces to a standstill in 1953, and it has repeatedly expressed its readiness to trade in any nuclear program it might have in order to secure it. That will was tested by the Clinton administration and, despite the common understanding to the contrary, North Korea kept to its bargain.

It is just over twenty years since President Reagan called the Soviet Union the "evil empire." If the "evil empire" of that epoch could become the (Russian) friend and partner of today, there is no reason to think that the same cannot happen with North Korea. For it to happen, however, rational calculation will have to be substituted for loathing, Pyongyang's legitimate grievances and fears will need to be addressed, the American-imposed division of the peninsula will have to be recognized as the original sin that is the ultimate cause of the contemporary Korean crisis, and "normal" relations will have to be opened between North Korea and the United States and between North Kroea and Japan. Such an outcome probably depends on countries with the greatest stake in a peaceful resolution—South Korea, Japan, China, and Russia—resisting American unilateral pressure and imposing some "reverse pressure" of their own, a process that is already obviously underway.

The United States under George W. Bush has certainly multilateralized the North Korea problem, but it is far from clear that it will produce the result Washington intends, irresistible pressure on Pyongyang to force it to yield. By ruling out a solution by force, the Beijing Conference powers have effectively checkmated Washington's possession of overwhelming military might. In the diffuse, regional frame that shows signs of emerging to replace the bilateral United States–North Korean confrontation, there is a possibilty of greater understanding and sympathy for the North Korean cry for relief than existed in the bilateral forum. The parties to the Beijing process have begun to push the United States to grant the sort of nonaggression guarantees and ultimately the diplomatic recognition that Pyongyang seeks.

George W. Bush's signal at the APEC meeting in Bangkok in late October 2003 that he would consider giving North Korea "security assurances, possibly in a written form," indicated that the combination of pressures on Washington was having an effect. If the Beijing powers simultaneously strengthen their cooperative relationships with North Korea, thereby reducing its sense of crisis and embattlement, they might well succeed in securing a halt to any nuclear program it may be embarked upon in the context of a far-reaching normalization of relations. That is also the path most likely to lead to the dismantling of the "garrison state," the de-nuclearization of the region, and the freeing of the North Korean people. Certainly it is the only route likely to avoid a bloodbath on the Korean peninsula and a dramtic reversal of plans for regional cooperation and development.

# VIII

# WAR OR PEACE?

"I think war is unnecessary, it's unthinkable and unfortunately it's entirely possible."[1] Since the UN's Maurice Strong reported in these terms to Secretary-General Kofi Annan in April 2003, the situation around North Korea has stabilized and the threat of war has receded, at least temporarily, thanks in the main to the substitution of the six-nation Beijing conference formula for the stark confrontation of the U.S.–North Korea bilateral relationship, but the stability is at best brittle. Influential voices in Washington insist that talks change nothing fundamental. They see North Korea as posing an "imminent danger of nuclear weapons being detonated in American cities," a threat that must in the last resort be met by force.[2] They are dubious about the current Bush strategem of relying on Chinese cooperation in concentrating pressure to enforce Pyongyang's submission and believe that "in short, we must be prepared to win a war, not execute a strike." These experts envisage the application of force "swifter and more devastating," on a scale five times greater than the "shock and awe" administered to Iraq (not 800 but 4,000 sorties a day). For them, it is not just North Korean weapons of mass destruction that are anathema but the system itself, which they see as utterly indefensible, or evil, needing to be swiftly overthrown by any means at hand so that the people laboring under its yoke can be freed. This might now be called the Iraqi Solution.

The idea of a nuclear attack on an American city is terrifying, and there can be no disputing the proposition that all possible steps should be taken to prevent anyone from executing such a threat. However, if a nuclear threat to an American city is an outrage, the truth is that a nuclear threat to any city, any people, is an outrage, and morality demands cooperation in removing such threats from all societies and peoples. When it comes to Korea, however, such a thought is beyond the bounds of imagination or sympathy of most American political or opinion leaders. Americans would be astonished to learn that the North has lived under precisely such a threat for almost its entire history as a state. Today, American concerns cannot be addressed without also meeting and responding to this North Korean concern. While the North has never issued any nuclear threat, or indeed any threat of aggression against any state (save, of course, South Korea, which it challenges for legitimacy as *the* Korean state), it was subject to the threat of nuclear attack, regularly rehearsed in war games, for forty years, until the Clinton administration in 1994 pledged that the United States would not employ nuclear weapons to attack a non-nuclear state. It was the reinstatement of the threat by George W. Bush in 2001 that precipitated the current and continuing crisis.

Both the United States and North Korea today seek and have an equal right to relief from the Damoclean sword of nuclear devastation. The fact that Americans have so little consciousness of themselves as the cause of another state's fear is a measure of the distance between the center and the peripheries of an empire.

Embattled and isolated, like Japan in the last stages of the Pacific War, North Korea is desperate to survive and gives signs of being ready to sacrifice almost anything provided it can cling to one core value. For Japan in 1945 it was the emperor, for North Korea today it means its *suryong*, or leader system, the guerrilla state myth as now preserved by Kim Jong Il. A 73-year-old Japanese woman recently commented, in the letters column of a major daily, on her sense of astonishment at finding there still existed a country where life so closely resembled the Japan of her prewar childhood:

> Although food was extremely scarce, we carefully committed to memory the varieties of edible weed, intent on developing bodies able to be of use in repaying our obligation to our lord emperor. On the first and eighth of every month, we recited from memory the Imperial Rescript on Education and vowed loyalty to our lord emperor. In the mornings and evenings, we made obeisance before the shrine at the school gate where the portrait of our lord emperor was revered. Yet in those times when we were so physically and emotionally straitened, still we believed that ours was the highest life, the best life.[3]

She reminds us that sixty years ago the United States fought against a far more dangerous east Asian state, whose rule was no less offensive than today's Kim Jong Il and whose overthrow even more fervently desired. Japanese emperor Hirohito was then worshipped, his image reverenced, his words treated as sacred script, and the state was equated with him and his family. After careful deliberation, however, when the war ended Washington decided that Hirohito would be preserved; indeed it insisted that his preservation be the very condition of democratic Japanese statehood. So the emperor was indeed preserved, but around him everything changed. Above all, the military threat was excised. The optimistic scenario for North Korea would be that it too is offered a similar, face-saving path as part of a similarly comprehensive process of reform. However, the capacity to imagine and empathize with the people of North Korea, even while rejecting the system (as does this woman who recognizes it all too well), seems to be missing in the United States.

Almost nobody outside Pyongyang has any wish to defend the North Korean regime. After misgoverning, manipulating, oppressing, and lying to its people for fifty years, the Kim family has forfeited any right to govern. It lacks credibility and increasingly lacks legitimacy because of its failure to provide its citizens with the basic conditions of existence. However, the matrix in which this state is embedded is complex, and responsibility for it is certainly far more diffuse than just one family. Twenty-two million people live in North Korea and, for better or for worse, many still identify to one degree or another with the only regime they have ever known. Although President Bush likes to assume that Kim Jong Il is a dictator without popular support, the CIA, according to a March 2003 *Washington Post* report, "retracted its assessment that there was a substantial opposition to the North Korean dictator."[4] As the Japanese people supported the Hirohito regime in 1945, so many North Korean people support the Kim Jong Il regime today. Even if there were a way by which cruise missiles and precision bombs could destroy all nuclear-related facilities without reducing much of North Korea to a smoking Chernobyl—which is far from clear—violence is incapable of delivering freedom to such people.

While Pyongyang now shows an unprecedented willingness for change and desire to engage with the capitalist system and is slowly, but most likely irrevocably, switching its economy to market principles, it is perverse of the United States to insist on full-scale, instantaneous "regime change." When George W. Bush professes especial outrage over North Korea's failure to feed its people, he forgets that North Korea was once an agricultural showcase, and he ignores the fact that famine and the collapse of the agricultural (and industrial) economy during the 1990s were at least partly due to factors beyond the control of the regime, including the long-continuing U.S.-led exclusion from world financial and technical markets, the collapse of "socialism" in neighboring Russia (the Soviet Union) and China, and a succession of natural disasters of unparalleled ferocity.

Unlike most states that are feared by neighbors, territorial aggrandizement and proselytism have never interested North Korea. Unlike Hirohito's Japan in the 1930s and 1940s, Kim Il Sung and Kim Jong Il's North Korea has not invaded its neighbors and has no territorial ambitions (other than the goal, shared with South Korea, of national reunification). It should be difficult to paint such a state, with its fundamentally modest goals of domestic happiness (two meals a day of white rice) as menacing, yet the *Juche* state tends to be regarded as if, bizarre and incomprehensible, it had somehow landed from Mars to challenge the world community by hanging up a nuclear weapons shingle.

It should be clear from the account in this book that North Korea is indeed an unusual, in some respects bizarre, state, but its people are the same people who have created the economic and political miracle of democratic South Korea. Their behavior is different because it has been determined by different recent historical experience. North Korea's founding fathers were, and to large extent still are, esteemed for having led the struggle for national independence and unity, first against Japan and then against the United States and its allies. For that, Kim Il Sung came to be revered as the North Korean equivalent of a George Washington. All the myths that sustain this state are myths of heroic resistance against enormous odds. Its worldview looks like an extreme form of paranoia but is sustained by real threat. Faced with that continuing threat,

North Koreans, like most people, will tend to unite around their leader. The partisan heroes of the anti-Japanese struggle of the 1930s are their inspiration. Only with the normalization of relations will the bitter history taught the North Korean people—that they must repel their enemies—be put into the background of consciousness.

What this means is that George W. Bush and Kim Jong Il stand in a paradoxically symbiotic relationship with each other. Bush's loathing for Kim, and his nuclear threat, maintains the isolation and siege conditions that help Kim legitimize his rule, mobilize nationalist support, and crush opposition. Bush, for his part, rules and reigns over northeast Asia because Japan and South Korea feel compelled by the North Korean threat to seek American protection, sheltering, in a fashion hardly less bizarre than anything in the *Juche* world, under Washington's "nuclear umbrella."

From being forced to watch and analyze every U.S. move, North Korea has learned a lesson that Washington would not wish it to avow: that the world, the United States above all, respects above all military might, and especially nuclear weapons and intercontinental missiles. It found that, although the United States would not talk to North Korea for forty years after the end of the Korean War, it suddenly agreed to talks in 1993 when the *Nodong* missile was launched, and it took the launch of the *Taepodong* satellite in 1998 to spur the Clinton administration to initiate the process of review that brought the two countries by October 2000 to the brink of normalization. Threatened and abused by the Bush administration, North Korea watched carefully the fate of Saddam Hussein's Iraq. It seems to have concluded that only possession of nuclear weapons could ensure its own survival. It determined therefore to trade away its nuclear assets, whatever they may be, only for irrevocable guaranties of security.

The North Korean threat is made up of nuclear weapons,

missiles, and possibly other kinds of WMD, together with the programs designed to produce and deploy them. For more than a decade, the United States insisted that North Korea had "one, possibly two" nuclear weapons. In 2003, however, U.S. intelligence shifted to adopt the South Korean, Russian, and Chinese view: that it actually did not have any at all. Instead, it told us that North Korea was working feverishly to develop them and might have them soon. It is almost certainly true that North Korea would like to have nuclear weapons, its own "deterrent," but it suspended its efforts to produce when it felt its security needs were satisfactorily met by the Agreed Framework, only changing course when the United States changed course with the advent of the Bush administration and the collapes of the Agreed Framework. As for missiles, the *Nodong* was successfully fired once, in 1993, while the longer-range *Taepodong* failed to achieve orbit and crashed into the ocean in 1998, and blew up on the launching pad in 2002 (according to South Korean intelligence); yet these modest efforts are enough to cause something akin to terror in Japan.

Pyongyang today shouts from the rooftops about its various programs, especially its nuclear deterrent and its processing of the waste fuel rods from the Yongbyon reactor to prepare plutonium for its weapons. But there is reason to think that it might protest too much and be resorting to bluff to try to gain the American attention it needs. North Korea declares that its reason for having nuclear weapons is exclusively defensive and professes its readiness, even eagerness, to trade them away provided it can secure thorough-going guarantees of its security and "normalization" of its relations with the world's major economic powers and international institutions.

However misguided one may think it, nuclear weapons are seen by Pyongyang as the path toward lifting the fifty-year siege. It has no other card to play, nothing to attract the attention of the superpower. Pyongyang continues to insist that it is prepared to satisfy all United States security concerns if only it is given guarantees of its own security. In 1994 it froze whatever programs it might have had and chose a diplomatic solution, and it declares its readiness to do the same again today.

Although Washington insists that Pyongyang broke its commitments by developing a covert uranium-enrichment program, that program, purchased (probably) in 1998 or 1999, seems to have been adopted as insurance against the possible collapse of the Agreed Framework. Until 2003 North Korea did not, apparently, actually enrich any uranium, much less produce any weapons. As for the Yangbyon reactor, the plutonium-generating programs and the reactor waste pools were frozen, as promised, between 1994 and 2003. It was the various threatening acts of the Bush administration—the inclusion on the nuclear target list and the "axis of evil" statement—that Pyongyang saw as a unilateral breach of the Framework (and of the NPT) and an explicit threat to its survival. With American promises of light-water reactors and economic and political normalization shown to be empty, North Korea no longer felt bound by its own commitments.

It is remarkable today that South Korea, which once fought a fratricidal war and has been locked in hostile military confrontation with the North ever since, now shows the least fear and most understanding of its neighbor and has chosen a path of cooperation in the belief that change is in the cards and any residual military threat is adequately contained. The black-and-white, good-and-evil, moralistic frame within which North Korea is represented as "evil" is alien to Seoul. While the United States attempts to enforce change by issuing demands and refusing negotiation, careless of face and confident of its ability to project massive force, South Korea's "Sunshine" approach stems from a vein of Confucian wisdom in which human nature is seen as complex but never evil and in which even the poor, desperate, and friendless are entitled to respect and not to have their pride and face belittled. In the evolving confrontation of 2003, neither the United States nor Japan seems prepared to make any concession to North Korean "face" or to see in historical context the pain and the sense of justice, however perverted, driving that country. As a result, the more pressure is ratcheted up to force Pyongyang's submission, the less likely it is to submit.

The strident tones of newsreaders on Pyongyang TV and the hype and rhetoric of its communiqués convey an image of bellicosity but are more likely signs of fear and exhaustion after decades of war mobilization, economic failure, and recurrent mass campaigns. Despite such talk, there have been plenty of signals of a desire to set aside the guerrilla model of secrecy, mobilization, absolute loyalty to the commander, and priority to the military, and pursue a Korean version of *perestroika*—in short, to come in from the cold.

Reform of any kind is impossible, however, under conditions of continuing high tension. Like South Korea, China shares with North Korea a cultural frame of ethics and morality and sees its own past in North Korea's present. Its sensitivity leads it to take steps to "steadily open North Korean eyes to the outside world and let them realize they are not the happiest people in the world, as their propaganda teaches them . . . The personality cult will not be there forever"—so says Xu Wenji, a Korea specialist in the provincial capital of Changchun, citing China's experience in the Mao Zedong era. Although the Chinese government will not compromise on its goal of a non-nuclear Korean peninsula, says Xu, China would prefer to act behind the scenes to persuade, not browbeat, in order that "the DPRK can still have some face left."[5] While U.S. and Japanese demands for change actually inhibit the possibility of change, Xu subtly suggests (and it is an apt description of Seoul's approach, too) that the best way to encourage change in the system is simply to encourage the conditions that will allow it. Russia as well has made clear its view that North Korea should be entitled to guarantee of its existence without having to plead for it. The best hope for a peaceful way forward today lies in these members of the Beijing conference group pressing that view on Washington. All are committed to a nonnuclear peninsula. None dare openly oppose the United States, but increasingly North Korea's four neighbor countries share certain basic principles, especially that North Korea's security problems are genuine and serious and that the problem must be resolved other than by force. Perhaps they also share the view, although only the Chinese would dare articulate it (as Wang Yi did after the August conference in Beijing), that the real problem is not so much North Korean, as American, attitudes and policies.

There are three possible outcomes to the present crisis. The first would be a deal whereby Pyongyang accepts the decommissioning of its reactors, removal of all plutonium and uranium-related facilities from the country, a return to the NPT regime and strict inspections in return for security guarantees and an economic package. This would follow along lines already familiar from the collapsed Agreed Framework. It would be close to what Pyongyang has repeatedly offered and the United States has thus far refused to consider. Timing of the implementation of such an agreement would be of the essence, with the United States wanting Pyongyang to make its commitments unilaterally before any other steps are initiated and Pyongyang seeking simultaneous and graduated implementation. Should such an agreement be reached, a prolonged period of uncertainty could still be anticipated as the pledges were implemented "in a verifiable and irreversible manner," but the regime in Pyongyang might continue.

In the second case, failure of negotiations could lead to the imposition of sanctions, whether or not pursuant to a Security Council resolution. Such an outcome would involve economic encirclement and steadily increasing pressure designed to enforce the abandonment of nuclear and missile programs. It would carry the risk of provoking North Korea, possibly to the point of launching a preemptive war. The sanctions path could only be contemplated if the cooperation of all four neighbor states was assured, something that seems at this point unlikely.

The third possibility is that of a fatal breakdown in negotiations leading to a U.S. or U.S.–led attack designed to destroy nuclear facilities, missile launching sites, and other related places and to overthrow the regime—to "win a war, not execute a strike." The "optimum" outcome of such a development—a quick military success—could only prove the most Pyhhric of victories. Depending on the degree of resistance that North Korea poses, and on whether or not it is even capable of launching a counterattack against South Korea, Japan, or both, casualties would be at least in the thousands, possibly in the tens of thousands, conceivably, if catastrophe strikes, in the millions. Physical devastation would be immense. The South Korean and possibly the Japanese economies would be subjected to huge strains, and much of the peninsula might be polluted by the depleted uranium-tipped "precision" weapons stocked by the U.S., with consequences for the environment and public health for generations to come—because depleted uranium's half life is 4.8 billion years.[6] Korea's "morning calm" would become something to be reconstructed by museums.

Beyond this gloomy prognosis for a "successful" war, there are other, complex ways in which an assault would disrupt and transform regional and global politics. Reluctant as it almost certainly would be about the resort to war, South Korea would find itself inheriting by "victory" (of which there can be no doubt) political dominance over the peninsula, large swathes of which could be devastated. Already, before any hostilities, anti-U.S. sentiment is strong in South Korea. After such a war such hostility would certainly increase. While the United States might think of war as the simple way to eliminate a hostile force in North Korea, it might find that instead it had created a much larger one in an angry, economically devastated but now-united Korea.

Under the Bush administration, the framework of U.S. military bases in east Asia is justified in Seoul and Tokyo by the threat from Pyongyang. Without the "North Korean threat," whether resolved peacefully or otherwise, Washington strategists would have to think of some new justification for the bases and for the massively expensive antimissile system to be constructed in Japan (or South Korea, or Australia). Some might want to declare China the real enemy, but a military alliance with the United States whose orientation was containment and hostility toward China would find little support in contemporary South Korea or Japan. Paradoxically, if the United States does accomplish what it wants in North Korea—regime change—it could find its own domination of the region undermined.

In 2003, both Japan and South Korea pledged their support to the U.S.–led occupation of Iraq, promising troops and, in the case of Japan, substantial funds. Yet it was plain that their real intent was not so much to share in a strategic vision as to do the superpower's bidding in order to ensure the United States's support in the event of any sudden crisis over North Korea. In South Korea, it was also announced in 2003 that U.S. forces would be redeployed away from the 38th parallel and their role converted from a "tripware"—to spark immediate U.S. involvement in the event of a Northern invasion of South Korea, into a highly mobile force for possible deployment as far away as central Asia or the Middle East. South Korean government consent to such a reorganization was based exclusively on the desire to keep the Americans in South Korea for purely Korean reasons, and so as not to destabilize the delicate

South-North military balance. In the words of a Chinese proverb, the United States's presence in both Japan and South Korea is a case of "sharing a bed but seeing different dreams." Although the Bush administration strives to eliminate the North Korean threat, paradoxically it is the very existence of that threat which facilitates the incorporation and subjection of these two major east Asian countries into America's Asian imperium.

Washington's post–Cold War vision involves asking Japan and Korea, in effect, to accept a future world predicated on hostility to either North Korea or China. Only that ensures their continuing dependence on the United States in military, political, and economic matters. Japan has been offered the role of the Britain of east Asia in such an order. For South Korea, or a united Korea, no clear role has yet been articulated, but whatever role is assigned would undoubtedly be secondary to Japan's, perhaps as a kind of east Asian Northern Ireland. Like Europe, however, the region has its own rhythms and its own dynamics. As in Europe, there is a deep, if complex, urge to move in the direction of mutual cooperation and self-reliance. Offered ongoing dependency on the United States, structured around bilateral treaty arrangements rather than any regional consensus, and marked by a base structure meant to last well into the next century, it is likely at some point to reply: "no thank you." Dependent alliances, born of circumstances half a century old when Japan was emerging from the humiliation of defeat and South Korea was a Cold War frontline state, locked in desperate poverty and almost total economic and political dependence, are no longer appropriate to a world in which Japan is an economic superpower, while South Korea constitutes a new model of economic growth and dwarfs its Northern rival in any measure but geographic size. Increasingly, voices may be heard in the region insisting it is past time to begin a multilateral, regional reconsideration of security issues, with an emphasis shifting gradually from military security to security founded in justice, human rights, and the satisfaction of basic human needs.

While U.S. regional and global policy offers only negative priorities—anti-terror, anti-"evil"—from east Asia there are tentative signs of the emergence of an alternative, nonimperial vision, not easily reconcilable with the Bush administration's vision of global domination. Beyond the gloom, anger, and rising tension of the "North Korean crisis" may be detected a process of east Asian evolution in a direction Europe has already taken. For over a decade a handful of Japanese and Korean scholars have been struggling to articulate such a vision.[7] They ask why east Asia failed to evolve a concert of states other than the Japanese-dominated "Greater East Asia Co-Prosperity Sphere" in the first half of the twentieth century and the U.S.-dominated "free world" in the second half; the former disastrous, the latter increasingly anomalous as the Cold War conditions that gave it birth disappear. Early in the twenty-first century, an externally oriented dependence still characterizes too much of east Asia's economic and security arrangements—dependence on American markets and security guarantees articulated in distinct, bilateral defense relationships with Japan, Taiwan, and South Korea. They look at the evolution of postwar Europe and ask why Asia should not now follow a similar path.

In the construction of what some describe as a "Common House of Northeast Asia," a web of security, economic, and environmental cooperation would bind the region. Korea, North and South, following a "rapprochement and a merger . . . on the basis of democracy," would constitute the core of a community comprising Japan, China, Russia, and the United States. The island areas of Taiwan, Okinawa, and the Kuriles, together with Hawaii, could form crucial nodes of cooperation and openness, representative of the immensely complex ethnic, religious, philosophical, and economic makeup of the region. It may seem a vague and idealistic dream, but it has a hard economic dimension, manifest in the evolution of the institutions of economic and financial cooperation in east Asia and the Pacific over the past decade. In the early 1990s, various proposals for Asian integration were blocked by U.S. suspicion and Japanese reluctance. In 1997, faced with the "Asian financial crisis," the idea of an "Asian IMF" was discussed but ran into the same barrier. By the end of the decade, however, it was plainly absurd that three east Asian countries—Japan, China and South Korea—held 70 percent of the world's dollars and yet were structurally dependent on Washington with no control over its vertiginously rising deficits. In June 2003, Asia's central bankers met in Chiang Mai to discuss the possibility of structural cooperation and the issuance of "Asian bonds" denominated in a basket of Asian currencies (yen, yuan, won, baht). The idea of an Asian currency, in due course to rival the dollar and the euro, began to seem less inconceivable. For China and Japan, the "Asian Community" idea holds that sort of attraction the European Community did for Germany and France, reducing for each the fear of regional domination by the other. For middle-sized countries like Korea and Thailand it offers the promise of a more significant role in the wider region.[8]

As in Europe, so too in Asia, a sense of the futility and horror of war and a desire to transcend the clashing nationalisms of the nineteenth and twentieth centuries feed a growing aspiration for some such vision. In 2002, the idea was for the first time given official endorsement when articulated in formal statements by the leaders of South Korea, North Korea, and Japan. The Pyongyang *Communiqué* of Koizumi and Kim Jong Il, along with the inaugural presidential speech of Roh Moo-Hyun, endorsed the idea of a Northeast Asian Community. When Kim and Koizumi spoke of the importance of "establishing cooperative relationships based upon mutual trust among countries in the region this was the first time in the nearly six decades since the collapse of Japan's ill-fated Co-Prosperity Sphere, that the goal of a regional community had been enunciated at the highest state level. That the proposition came in a joint statement with the leader of North Korea gave it added significance. South Korean president Roh in his twenty-minute inauguration speech included no less than seventeen references to the concept of "northeast Asia." He looked to a future in which one could go to the railway station in Pusan at the tip of the Korean peninsula to buy a ticket for Paris, via Seoul and Pyongyang, across China, Mongolia, and Russia.[9] In Beijing in July 2003, he spoke again of the path by which east Asia would emulate the European Union where "walls of suspicion" that once divided a continent had crumbled.[10] European precedent suggests that some, at least, of the institutions of such a community would be located on Korean soil, following the model of European preference for the location of core institutions in smaller countries, such as Luxembourg and Belgium.

The twentieth century began and ended in tragedy for Korea, incorporated into the world order of imperialism as a colonial dependency, divided, plunged into a civil war that became a surrogate world war, militarized, and possibly nuclearized. Early in the twenty-first century the outlook is far from bright, but so many unresolved contradictions are concentrated on the Korean peninsula that it now attracts global attention. War is unthinkable, the ultimate expression of a failure of the human spirit, and the legitimate interests of the parties are not in fundamental opposition. A solution should not be unattainable. North Korea says it does not want nuclear weapons provided only that its security is guaranteed. The United States says it will address North Korea's concerns only after it abandons its nuclear programs. It should require no genius to bridge such a gap, while resort to war by either party would be criminal. Once a peaceful way forward is found through the present crisis, it holds the promise of unlocking the potential for the construction of a new, truly twenty-first-century Asia, in which the legacies of the previous two centuries are at last resolved.

Any freedom delivered by cruise missile would be ephemeral at best, while normalization of relations in the region will open the way to the liberation of the North Korean people. In close collaboration with their compatriots to the south, they will choose, when windows are opened around them, what government and what ideology they believe will best serve them. War could not solve anything fifty years ago, and all that has changed since then is that its destructive force has been immeasurably increased.

# NOTES

## CHAPTER 1

1. Bob Woodward, *Bush at War*, New York, Simon and Schuster, 2002, p. 340.
2. Meeting with Republican senators, May 2002, Howard Fineman, "I sniff some politics," *Newsweek* (U.S. edition), May 27, 2002.
3. "The case against the war," *The Nation*, February 13, 2003.
4. Marcus Noland, *Avoiding the Apocalypse: The Future of the Two Koreas*, International Economic Institute, 2000, p. 350.
5. "Newsstation," TV Asahi, June 20, 2003.
6. The well-known Japanese commentator, Funabashi Yoichi, makes an analogy with the snail instead of the porcupine—recoiling into its shell at the slightest contact with unexpected objects. (Funabashi Yoichi, "KEDO to iu gaiko tejina," *Asahi shimbun*, July 3, 2003.)
7. British parliamentarian Glyn Ford reports on the dialogue between North Korea and the EU on human rights matters: Glyn Ford, " 'Neocon' recipe for disaster," *Japan Times*, July 5, 2003.
8. Peter Hayes, "Last chance to avert a Korean Krakatoa," Nautilus Institute, Nautilus Policy Forum Online, August 11, 2003.
9. UNICEF Briefing Note, Beijing, March 11, 2003.

## CHAPTER 2

1. Stewart Lone and Gavan McCormack, *Korea Since 1850*, New York, St. Martin's Press, 1993, p. 96.

2. Mark Gayn, *Japan Diary*, Tokyo, 1982, p. 263.

3. Charles Armstrong, *The North Korean Revolution*, 1945–1950, Ithaca and London, Cornell University Press, 2003, pp. 241, 245.

4. Against Canadian and Australian opposition. See Australian Delegation to the United Nations to Department of External Affairs, Cablegram, 24 February 1950, http://www.info.dfat. gov.au/info/historical/HistDocs.nsf/vVolume/DE97D896985 C1853CA256CD9001653EA . See also Leon Gordenker, *The United Nations and the Peaceful Unification of Korea, The Politics of Field Operations, 1947–1950*, The Hague, 1969, p. 71.

5. K.P.S. Menon, *Many Worlds: An Autobiography*, London, 1965, p. 259.

6. Ralph Harry (of Australia's Department of External Affairs), *Cold War Hot War*, p. 46.

7. On Cheju, see John Merrill, 'The Cheju-do Rebellion,' *Journal of Korean Studies*, vol. 2, 1980, pp. 139–97. For a brief account, see also Bruce Cumings, *Korea's Place in the Sun—A Modern History*, New York, W.W. Norton, 1997, pp. 217–222.

8. Kathryn Wethersby, "New findings on the Korean war, translation and commentary," Cold War International History Project (hereafter CWIHP), 1993, http://www.seas.gwu.edu/ nsarchive/cwihp.

9. (Australia's) Patrick Shaw, dispatch from Tokyo, 12 July 1949, quoted McCormack, *Cold War Hot War*, p. 57.

10. Quoted in Bruce Cumings, *The Origins of the Korean War*, 2 vols, Princeton University Press, 1981 and 1990, vol 2, p. 227.

11. Department of External Affairs to Washington (Australian Embassy), cable, 24 March 1949, McCormack, *Cold War Hot War*, p. 56.

12. Kathryn Wethersby, cit.

13. Chen Jian, "The Sino-Soviet alliance and China's entry into the Korean War," Cold War International History Project, Working Paper No. 1, 1992, CWIHP virtual archive.

14. NHK shuzaihan, *Chosen senso*, Tokyo, 1990, pp. 94–95.

15. Trygve Lie. *In the Cause of Peace: Seven, Years with the United Nations*, New York, 1954, p. 329.

16. McCormack, *Cold War Hot War*, p. 75.

17. For detailed discussion, see McCormack, *Cold War Hot War*, pp. 75–84.

18. Jon Halliday and Bruce Cumings, *Korea—The Unknown War*, London and New York, Penguin Viking, 1988, p. 73.

19. "United States Objectives and Programs for National Security, 14 April 1950," Thomas Etzold and John Lewis Gaddis, eds., *Containment: Documents on American Policy and Strategy, 1945–1950*, New York, 1978, pp. 385–87; see also discussion in Cumings, *The Origins of the Korean War*, vol. 2, pp. 177–81.

20. Anatoly Torkunov, *The War in Korea 1950–1953, Its Origin, Bloodshed and Conclusion*, Tokyo, ICF Publishers, 2000, p. 88.

21. Lobov, quoted in NHK, p. 107; see also Jon Halliday, "Air operations in Korea: The Soviet side of the story," William J. Williams, ed, *A Revolutionary War—Korea and the Transformation of the Postwar World*, Chicago, Imprint Publications, 1993.

22. Halliday and Cumings, p. 132.

23. The unit was under the command of Okubo Takeo, later Rear-Admiral. (Okubo Takeo, *Uminari no hibi*, Tokyo, 1978, and interviews with the author, Tokyo, 1981.)

24. Joseph C. Goulden, *Korea: the Untold Story of the War*, New York, 1982, p. 49.

25. Cumings, *Korea's Place in the Sun*, pp. 290–1.

26. William Stueck, *Rethinking the Korean War: A New Diplomatic and Strategic History*, Princeton and Oxford, Princeton University Press, 2002, p. 165.

27. Callum MacDonald, *Korea: The War Before Vietnam*, Houndmills and London, MacMillan, 1986, p. 132.

28. Ibid., p. 177.

29. Ibid., p. 179.

30. Detailed sources for the following brief account may be

found in McCormack, *Cold War Hot War*, pp. 147–158, or in Lone and McCormack, pp. 115–118.

31. Halliday and Cumings, pp. 128–29.

32. See the various articles by Milton Leitenberg and Kathryn Wethersby, under the auspices of the Cold War International History Project at the Woodrow Wilson Center in Washington, published in the *Cold War International History Project Bulletin*, and reproduced on the web at: http://www.seas.gwu. edu/nsarchive/cwihp. See also Milton Leitenberg, "Resolution of the Korean War biological warfare allegations," *Critical Reviews in Microbiology*, Vol. 24, No. 3, 1998, pp. 169–194, where the documents are quoted in full.

33. Quoted in Halliday and Cumings, p. 185.

34. Henry Kissinger, *Nuclear Weapons and Foreign Policy*, New York, Harper and Brothers, 1957, p. 376.

35. See discussion in McCormack, Cold War Hot War, pp. 151–154.

36. MacDonald, pp. 234–5.

37. Walter Karig, Malcolm Cagle and Frank A. Manson, *Battle Report: The War in Korea*, New York, 1952, pp. 111–112.

38. MacDonald, p. 234.

39. Cumings, *Korea's Place in the Sun*, p. 294.

40. MacDonald, p. 235.

41. Wada Haruki, *Chosen senso zenshi (Complete History of the Korean War)*, Tokyo, Iwanami, 2002, p. 370.

42. Ibid., p. 391.

43. MacDonald, p. 241.

44. Park Myung-lim [Pak Myong-nim], *Han'guk 1950: Chonjaeng-gwa P'yonghwa* (Korea 1950: War and Peace), Seoul, Nanam, 2002, p. 324. (According to Park, these orders were issued "at the highest levels" and were not limited by geographical area.)

45. Ambassador Muccio to U.S. 8th Army commander Lt. General Walton L. Walker, August 25, 1950, Sang-hun Choe, "Wit-

nesses, 1950 documents say S. Koreans shot thousands of prisoners," Associated Press, April 21, 2000, http://www.wire. ap.org/Appackages/nogunri/executions.html.

46. Gregory Henderson, *Korea: The Politics of the Vortex*, Cambridge, Mass., 1968, p. 167.

47. William F. Dean, *General Dean's Story*, London, 1954, p. 68.

48. John Riley and Wilbur Schramm, *The Reds take a City: The Communist Occupation of Seoul, with Eyewitness Accounts*, New Brunswick, 1951, pp. 35, 65–7, 118.

49. Cumings, *The Orgins of the Korean War*, vol 2, pp. 668–73.

50. See McCormack, *Cold War Hot War*, pp. 141–2 for the evidence of the UN military observer team concerning massacres thought to have been carried out by both sides during the Northern retreat and Southern reoccupation of territory adjacent to the Han River at Yanpyong and Tupori to the north of Seoul in September–October 1950.

51. Park, pp. 614–5.

52. T. R. Fehrenbach, *This Kind of War*, London, 1963, pp. 200–201.

53. Cumings, *The Origins of the Korean War*, vol 2, p. 702.

54. Ibid., p. 719.

55. Ibid., p. 282.

56. Ibid., p. 721.

57. "Korean Historical Report," War Crimes Division, Judge Advocate Section, Korean Communications Zone, APO 234, Cumulative to 30 June 1953, copy in Australian Archives, Victorian division, MP 729/8, Department of the Army, Classified Correspondence Files, 1945–1957, File 66/431/25.

58. See, for example, *Daily Telegraph* (Sydney), October 30, 1953.

59. Park, p. 324.

60. Extract from the Peach/Rankin report carried in Dispatch by A. B. Jamison, Head of Australian Mission in Tokyo, to Canberra, 10 August 1950, Australian Archives 3123/5, Part 4.

61. Peach, interview with author, Sydney, August 14, 1982.

62. Rankin confirmed this account in an August 12, 1982, interview with the author by referring to his 1950 diary.

63. Stephen Simmons (journalist) and photographer Haywood Magee, "War in Korea," Picture Post, vol 48, No. 5, July 1950, p. 17. (The caption describes the incident as a matter "which has been investigated by a United Nations observer.")

64. Philip Deane, *Captive in Korea*, London, 1953, p. 83. (The 1953 U.S. Army report locates the headquarters of the North Korean forces it alleged were responsible for the September massacre in "the Catholic mission" in Taejon.)

65. Park, p. 324 (quoting from U.S. National Archives).

66. No Ka-Won, "Taejon hyongmuso sachon sanbaek myong haksal sakon" (The massacre of 4,300 men from the Taejon prison), *Mal*, February 1992, pp. 122–31.

67. Park (p. 337) concludes from his analysis of various sources, including the North Korean report in *Chosun Inminho* of August 10, 1950, that 400 people were killed at Nogunri between July 26 and 29.

68. Elizabeth Becker, "Army confirms G.I.'s in Korea killed civilians," *New York Times*, January 12, 2001. The full report of the official investigation, "No Gun Ri Review" is available on the web, http://www.army.mil/nogunri/. The authors of the original investigative report won a Pulitzer for it and subsequently published it as a book; Charles J. Hanley, Sang-Hun Choe, and Martha Mendoza, *The Bridge at No Gun Ri—A Hidden Nightmare from the Korean war*, New York, Henry Holt, Owl Books, 2002. A fine television documentary was also made of it by the BBC: "Timewatch: Kill 'em all," January 31, 2002. See also Bruce Cumings, "Occurrence at Nogun ri Bridge: An enquiry into the history and memory of a civil war," *Critical Asian Studies*, vol. 33, No. 4, November 2001, pp. 509–526.

69. Quoted in NHK, p. 205.

70. Evan Luard, *A History of the United Nations*, Vol. 1, *The Years of Western Dominance*, 1945–1955, London, 1982, p. 263.

71. On the POW issue, MacDonald, pp. 134–146; see also Wada, *Chosen senso zenshi*, p. 342.

72. Admiral C. Turner Joy, *How Communists Negotiate*, New York, 1955, p. 152.

73. Gavan McCormack, "Wilfred Burchett's Thirty Year War: Korea" in Ben Kiernan (ed.), *The Other Side of the World: The Reporting of Wilfred Burchett*, 1939–1983, London, Quartet Books, 1986, pp.162–211.

74. Halliday and Cumings, p. 178.

75. McCormack, "Wilfred Burchett's Thirty Years War, Korea," p. 175.

76. Rosemary Foot, *A Substitute for Victory: The Politics of Peacemaking at the Korean Armistice Talks*, Ithaca and London, Cornell University Press, 1990, p. 191.

77. Wada, *Chosen senso zenshi*, p. 464.

78. On their subsequent fate: Foot, p. 196.

79. McCormack, "Wilfred Burchett's Thirty Years War, Korea," p. 179.

80. Halliday and Cumings, p. 180; McCormack, *Cold War Hot War*, pp. 142–5.

81. Halliday and Cumings, p. 176.

82. Department of External Affairs, Canberra, to Australian Mission (New York), 3 November 1953. Australian Archives, A1 838/T184, 3123/5/7/2, pt 1.

83. Halliday and Cumings, p. 181.

84. Halliday and Cumings, pp. 187, 197; Wada, *Chosen senso zenshi*, pp. 433ff.

85. MacDonald, p. 192.

86. Foot, p. 191.

87. Park, pp. 743–6; Kathryn Wethersby, "North Korea and the Big Brother," Minnesota Public Radio, July 2003, http://www.americannetworks.org/features/korea/c6.html .

88. Ben Fenton, 'Korean War deaths cut," *Daily Telegraph*, 5 June 2000 (citing Pentagon sources).

**CHAPTER 3**

1. Wada Haruki, *Kin Nissei to Manshu kinichi senso* (Kim Il Sung and the Manchurian resistance war against Japan), Heibonsha, 1992.

2. On Pochombo, ibid, pp. 185ff.

3. Bruce Cumings, *The Origins of the Korean War*, 2, vols, 1981 and 1990, Princeton University Press, vol. 1, p. 402.

4. For a detailed discussion of the public security system in the early decades, see Robert Scalapino and Chong-Sik Lee, *Communism in Korea*, 2 vols., University of California Press 1972, vol. 2, The Society, pp. 818 ff.

5. Charles A. Armstrong, "Revolution, subjectivity and self-reliance: North Korea and the world, 1945–2002," Unpublished paper, Cornell University, New York, September 26, 2002.

6. *Nodong shinmun*, quoted in Far Eastern Economic Review, July 4, 1975.

7. *The Path of Great Love*, Pyongyang, FLPH, 1977, p. 139.

8. "Introduction," NKnet (Network for North Korean Democracy and Human Rights), http://www.nknet.org/en/book-introduction.php.

9. Quoted in Marcus Noland, *Avoiding the Apocalypse: The Future of the Two Koreas*, Washington, D.C., Institute for International Economics, 2000, p. 62.

10. Konstantin Pulikovsky, *Vostochnii Ekspress: Po Rossii's Kim Chen Irom* (Orient Express: Across Russia with Kim Jong Il), Moscow, Gorodets, 2002, p. 46.

11. John Gorenfeld, "The producer from hell," *The Guardian*, April 4, 2003.

12. Quoted in Kamoura Motoaki, "Chosen hanto yuji wa aru no ka," *Manga de wakatta Kita Chosen mondai*, Tokyo, Maiwei shuppan, 2003, pp. 92–99, at p. 98. The major locus for their story is: Choi Eun-hee and Shin Sang-ok, *Yami kara no kodama—ratchi, kankin, toso* (Echoes from the Darkness—

abduction, detention, escape), Tokyo, 2 vols., Ikeda shoten, 1988–9.

13. "Film Guru Shin Sang Ok Tells of Kim Jong Il," *Seoul Times*, November 2001.

14. His casual self-deprecatory references to his stature suggest a particular sensitivity. For the record, Shin and Choi gave his height as 163 cm. North Korean diplomats commonly give 170 cms. South Koreans estimate it at 167 cm, and Kim Dae Jung came away from his 2000 meeting estimating his counterpart to be 173 cm. (Pulikovsky, *Vostochnii Ekspress*, p. 145.) Napoleon is said to have been 168 cm (five foot six inches in British measure).

15. Choi and Shin, vol. 2, p. 279.

16. Choi and Shin, vol. 2, p. 82.

17. Konstantin Pulikovsky, special representative of Russian president Putin to the Far East Federal District, "Book to shed light on Kim's visit to Russia," *Vladivostok News*, March 26, 2003. For Pulikovsky's detailed account, *Vostochnii Ekspress*.

18. Pulikovsky, *Vostochnii Ekspress*, p. 59.

19. David R. Sands, "Kim Jong Il's appetites are ingredients of book," *Washington Times*, July 9, 2003. See Fujimoto Kenji, *Kim Jong Il no ryorinin*, Tokyo, Fusosha, 2003.

20. Ijuin, p. 172.

21. Alexandre Y. Mansourov, "Korean Monarch Kim Jong Il: Technocrat ruler of the hermit kingdom facing the challenges of modernity," Nautilus Institute, The DPRK Briefing Book, 2003.

22. Summarized from the discussion at Sung Hae Rang, *Kita Chosen Harukanari-Kita Chosen kantei de kurashita 20 nen*, Tokyo, Bunshun bunko, 2003, pp. 400–401. For a recent interview with Ms. Sung: Adriana Lee, "Secret Lives," *Time*, June 30, 2003, pp. 28–33.

23. Sung, pp. 413, 421–3, 458, 471, 500.

24. Ijuin, p. 200.

25. " 'Kim's son' tried Tokyo's soaplands," *Japan Today*, May 21, 2003.

26. His ring-name was "Daidozan Matamichi." (Kin Jon-il soshoki no tsuma no chichi wa puroresura," *Tokyo Sports*, July 10, 2003.)

27. Wada Haruki, *Kita Chosen—Yugekitai kokka no genzai*, Iwanami shoten, 1998, pp. 141ff.

28. Andrew C. Nahm, *North Korea Today: Her Past, Reality and Impression*, Kalamazoo, 1978, p. 86.

29. Aidan Foster-Carter, "North Korea: Development and Self-Reliance: A Critical Reappraisal," in Gavan McCormack and Mark Selden, eds., *Korea North and South: The Deepening Crisis*, New York, Monthly Review Press, 1978, p. 123.

30. On Juche (sometimes Chuche), see Han S. Park, *North Korea—The Politics of Unconventional Wisdom*, Boulder and London, Lynne Rienner, 2002. See also Wada Haruki, Kita Chosen, pp. 150ff.

31. Kim Il Sung, "On the Thirtieth Anniversary of the Korean Workers' Party," October 9, 1975, Pyongyang, FLPH, 1975.

32. Speeches by Li Jong Ryong, president of Kumsong Political University, and U Dal Ho, director of the Kim Il Sung Party Academy, Pyongyang, March 1982, in *People's Korea*, April 17, 1982, p. 5.

33. Wada, *Kin Nissei to Manshu konichi senso*, pp. 6ff; Adrian Buzo, *The Guerrilla Dynasty: Politics and Leadership in North Korea*, St. Leonards, New South Wales, Allen and Unwin, 1999.

34. Wada, Kita Chosen, pp. 294–5.

35. Taken, with slight adaptation to the wording, from NKnet, http://www.nknet.org/enknet/ekeys/ekeys6/e-606.htm.

36. Saito Ichiro, ed., *Kim Jong Il dokusai kokka no shotai*, Tokyo, Tama shuppan, 2003, pp. 116–7.

37. Haruhisa Ogawa, "Correlation between Juche ideology and political prison camps in North Korea," paper presented at

First International Conference on North Korean Human Rights and Refugees, Seoul, 1999, http://www.chosun-journal.com/haruhisaogawa.html.

38. In the early 1960s there were only two such prison camps, but as the imposition of the "monolithic ideology" and the succession of Kim Jong Il proceeded, many more had to be opened. By 1990 there were about twenty such camps. (Yun Dae-il, *Kita Chosen kokka anzen hoeibu—Kim ocho o sasaeru kyofu no jinmin yokuatsu shisutemu*, Tokyo, Bungei shunjusha, 2003, translated by Hagiwara Ryo, p. 37.)

39. Thomas Omestad, "Gulag Nation: Unseen by the outside world, North Korea runs vast prison camps of unspeakable cruelty," *U.S. News and World Report*, June 23, 2003.

40. Yun Dae-il, pp. 40, 192. See also Kang Chol-Hwan and Pierre Rigoulot, *The Aquariums of Pyongyang—Ten years in the North Korean Gulag*, translated from French by Yair Reiner, New York, Basic Books, 2001.

41. Yun Dae-il, p. 76.

42. Lone and McCormack, p. 182.

43. Yun Dae-il, pp. 197–8.

44. *People's Korea*, April 17, 1982, p. 5.

45. Sheila Miyoshi Yager, "A Vision for the Future; or Making Family History in Contemporary South Korea," *Positions*, Vol. 4, No. 1, Spring 1996, pp. 31–58, especially p. 53.

46. Seki Hiroharu (former Tokyo University professor and leading figure in Japanese peace studies), presentation to the International Political Studies Association Conference, Seoul, August 1997. For an earlier articulation of this position see Seki Hiroharu, "Atarashii kokusai seiji o hiraku Juche shiso," *Kim Il Sung shugi kenkyu* (Studies in Kimilsungism, Tokyo, Journal of the Japan Studies in Kimilsungism Society), No. 53, April 1990, pp. 113–125.

47. Han S. Park, p. 63.

48. Han S. Park, pp. 75–82.

49. According to Choi and Shin, vol. 2, p. 268.

50. Deputy Prime Minister Kim Dal Hyon, quoted in Simon Darlin, "North Korea opens cautiously to the West," *Asian Wall St. Journal*, May 13, 1992.

51. Nishibori Tekemichi, "Daigaku kyoju, kokan, kyosei shuyojo kanbu made nigehajimeta," *Shukan Asahi*, February 7, 2003.

52. Jae Jean Suh, "Class conflict and regime crisis in North Korea," IPSA Conference, Seoul, August 1997.

**CHAPTER 4**

1. Ijuin Atsushi, *Kim Jong Il "Kaikaku" no kyojitsu*, Nihon keizai shimbunsha, 2002, pp. 103, 109.

2. Joan Robinson, "Korean Miracle," *Collected Economic Papers*, Oxford, B. Blackwell, 5 vols., 1951–1979, vol. 3, p. 208.

3. Gordon White, "North Korean Chuch'e: The Political Economy of Independence," *Bulletin of Concerned Asian Scholars*, vol. 7, No. 2, April–June 1975, pp. 44–54, at pp. 49, 52.

4. Aidan Foster-Carter, "North Korea: Development and Self-Reliance: A Critical Appraisal," Gavan McCormack and Mark Selden, eds., *Korea North and South: The Deepening Crisis*, New York, Monthly Review, 1978, pp. 115–149.

5. United States Central Intelligence Agency, National Foreign Assessment Center, *Korea: The Economic Race between the North and the South* (ER 78-100008), Washington DC, 1978.

6. FAO, *Yearbook-Production*, vol. 44, 1990, Rome 1991, table 17, p. 73.

7. Ibid., table 106, pp. 290–1. Revised figures in the 1991 volume at p. 238.

8. Wada Haruki, *Kita Chosen*, pp. 266ff.

9. "Hakubai no yume—hokai shita shutai noho—Kita Chosen no sugao (3), Keizai (2)," *Asahi shimbun*, July 23, 2003.

10. Hazel Smith, "Overcoming Humanitarian Dilemmas in the

DPRK (North Korea)," United States Institute of Peace, Washington, Special Report No. 90, July 2002, and also Smith's presentation, "Media myths and the DPRK," to Foreign Correspondents' Club of Japan, Tokyo, May 29, 2003.

11. Kim Jae-ho, "UN Warns of Aid Shortage for North Korea," *Chosun Ilbo*, December 9, 2003.

12. Smith, "Media Myths."

13. Ijuin, p. 88.

14. Joseph S. Chung, "Economy of North Korea," *The Far East and Australasia* 1990, London, 1989, p. 539.

15. See Paik Nak-chung, *Chosen hanto toitsuron*, Tokyo, Kurein, 2001, p. 51.

16. Bank of Korea estimate, *News Review* (Seoul), August 22, 1992, p. 15.

17. Noland, p. 79.

18. Smith, "Overcoming Humanitarian Dilemmas."

19. Estimates by Nautilus Institute and Korea Energy Economic Institute (KEEI), quoted by Barbara Demick, "N. Korea curses the dark," *Los Angeles Times*, February 11, 2003.

20. Mao Fang, "Chugoku-Kita Chosen kankei ni henka wa aru ka," *Sekai*, May 2003, pp. 155–163, at p. 159.

21. Wada, *Kita Chosen*, pp. 234–6 (the 2,000 days refers to the period when all stops were pulled out in the effort to reach the targets set by the 1987–93 Plan).

22. Foster-Carter, p. 140 (footnote).

23. Wada, *Kita Chosen* p. 238.

24. Ko Yong-hwan, *Pyongyang 25 ji—Kita Chosen bomei kokan no kokuhaku*, Tokuma bunko, 1997. (Ko was first secretary of the DPRK embassy in Congo until he defected in 1991.)

25. "Ratsiraka: 'Big man' cut to size," BBC News, July 5, 2002.

26. Inagaki Takeshi, *Kita Chosen ni tsukareta hitobito*, PHP, 2003, p. 150.

27. From 1997 speech, quoted in Noland, p. 85.

28. Ijuin, p. 43.

29. Wada, Kita Chosen, pp. 244–5, 252.

30. Ijuin, p. 57.

31. Ibid., p. 64.

32. Marcus Noland, *Avoiding the Apocalypse: The Future of the Two Koreas*, Washington, D.C., Institute for International Economics, 2000, p. 139.

33. *Asahi shimbun*, 15 July 2003.

34. Quoted at "Pyongyang Square": http://www.pyongyang-suare.com/economy/sinuiju.html.

35. "Hyundai Asan's inter-Korean cooperative business," Hyundai Corporation, Seoul, July 2003. (*Chosunjok*, or ethnic Koreans with Chinese citizenship and fluency in both Chinese and Korean, would be employed at $220 a month for simple tasks and $330 for bus drivers and the like, on top of free accommodation and fares, according to a Hyundai Asan official, interviewed in Seoul, July 8, 2003.)

36. Hyundai Asan official, op. cit.

37. Ibid.

38. Estimated at ca $148 million per year. Ijuin, p. 78.

39. Ijuin, p. 13.

40. 'Shijo no kaze, kasegi de hyoka himpu kakudai," Kita Chosen no sugao (3), Keizai (1), *Asahi shimbun*, July 22, 2003.

41. Furuya Koichi, "Kita Chosen—'yami ichiba o seishiki shonin,' " *Asahi shimbun*, June 8, 2003.

42. Maxim Kozlov (quoting Kim Yong Nam), "What's in a word? Reforms and the DPRK," *DPRK Business News Bulletin* (Beijing), Vol. 4, No. 27, July 2, 2003.

43. "Pyongyang eases control of center as West applies pressure," *Asian Wall St. Journal*, June 20, 2003.

44. Yoshiharu Asano, "N. Korean missile exports earned $580 million in '01," Daily Yomiuri Online, May 13, 2003.

45. Yun Dae-il, p. 252.

46. Hwang Jang Yop, "Hwang Jang Yop speaks," NKNET (Net-

work for North Korean Democracy and Human Rights),
http://www.nis.go.kr/eng/north/defector_index.html.

47. Nomura Hataru, ed., *Kita Chosen riken no shinso*, Bessatsu Takarajima, No. 049, 2003, p. 127.

48. Noland, p. 119.

49. Nomura Hataru, p. 127.

50. Richard Paddock and Barbara Demick, "North Korean drug smugglers take aim at Australia," *Japan Times*, June 5, 2003.

51. Shigemura Toshimitsu, *Kita Chosen'tte donna kuni?*, Tokyo, PHP, 2003, pp. 38–9.

52. Ah-Young Kim, "A narcotic state," *International Herald Tribune*, June 18, 2003.

53. Pulikovsky, pp. 131–2.

54. Alexandre Y. Mansourov, "Korean monarch Kim Jong Il: technocrat ruler of the hermit kingdom facing the challenge of modernity," Nautilus Instiute, The DPRK Briefing Book, July 2003.

55. Quoted in Sakajiri Nobuyoshi, "Shikigin shimeage e—misairu, mayaka soshi nerau," *Asahi shimbun*, June 3, 2003.

56. Noland, p. 121.

57. Ko Yong-hwan, quoted in Francis Deron, "China's dilemma as North Korea holds out the begging bowl," *Le Monde*, October 9, 1991. For a more detailed statement from Ko, Fan Min-Gi, ed, *Kin Nissei chosho* (Kim Il Sung file), Kobunsha, 1992, pp. 250–303.

58. Wada, *Kita Chosen*, p. 208.

## CHAPTER 5

1. Haksoon Paik, "What to do with the ominous cloud over the Korean peace process?" Northeast Asia Peace and Security Network, special report, February 19, 2002, ftp://ftp.nautilus.org/napsnet/special_reports/paik_DPRKbush.txt.

2. "North Korean economic survey team to visit South Korea," AP, Seoul, October 24, 2002.

3. $10,013 in South Korea and $762 in North Korea in 2002, according to the Unification Ministry in Seoul. ("Kita chosen kiki 50 nenme no kincho (3) Kokuron wareru Kankoku," *Nihon keizai shimbun*, 25 July 2003.)

4. Paik Nak Chung, "Habermas on National Unification in Germany and Korea," *New Left Review*, No. 121, September–October 1996, p. 18.

5. Victor Cha and David C. Kang, "The Korea Crisis," *Foreign Policy*, May–June 2003, pp. 20–28, at p. 24.

6. Financial Times, November 8, 2002.

7. Lim Dong Woon, South Korean presidential envoy, quoted in Joseph Coleman, "South Korea struggles with diplomatic role," AP, Seoul, January 30, 2003.

8. Kiyoshi Hasaba, "Resume Japan—N. Korea talks anytime possible," *Asahi shimbun*, February 8, 2003.

9. "South Korea stopped US strike on North Korea: former president," Agence France Presse, Seoul, May 24, 2000.

10. Don Oberdorfer, *The Two Koreas: A Contemporary History*, London 1998, p. 324.

11. "Possible high casualties mute war talk versus North Korea," *The Korea Herald*, December 19, 2002.

12. "The Two Koreas," *Newsweek*, December 23, 2002.

13. Howard French, "Seoul vote hinges on relations with north," *International Herald Tribune*, December 19, 2002.

14. Quoted, BBC, September 25, 2003.

15. Chalmers Johnson, "Korea, South and North, at Risk," Japan Focus, April 2003, http://www.japanfocus.org/032.html.

16. Kamoura Motoaki, "Chosen hanto yuji wa aru no ka," Himuki Fuminori, ed, *Manga de wakatta Kita Chosen mondai*, Tokyo, Maiwei shuppan, 2003, pp. 92–99, at p. 93.

17. Richard Perle (interview), "Kokuren ni chikara mo ishi mo nai, Kita Chosen ni wa 'atsuryoku'," *Asahi shimbun*, May 1, 2003.

18. Kamoura, p. 93.

19. Sir Hugh Cortazzi (British ambassador to Japan, 1980–84),

"Pyongyang—Keep the gloves on for now," Japan Times, July 2, 2003.

20. "Military comes first—no matter what," *Asahi shimbun*, June 28–29, 2003.

21. Colin Robinson and Stephen H. Baker, "Stand-Off with North Korea: War Scenarios and Consequences," Center for Defense Information, Washington, May 9, 2003, http://www.cdi.org/index.cfm. See also John Feffer, "Is North Korea Next?" *Foreign Policy in Focus*, March 24, 2003, and Chalmers Johnson, "Korea, South and North, at Risk."

22. Charles P. Vick, "Nodong," Federation of American Scientists, updated May 13, 2003, http://www.fas.org/nuke/guide/dprk/missile/nd-1.htm.

23. John Pike, Director of the Federation of American Scientists' space program, quoted in "Satellite photos show N. Korean launch site to be primitive," *Korea Times*, January 12, 2000.

24. Webmaster and Tim Brown, "No-dong, N40°51'17" E129°39'58", Federation of American Scientists, updated March 25, 2000, http://www.fas.org/nuke/guide/facility/nodong.htm.

25. Webmaster and Tim Brown, cit.

26. Leon V. Sigal, "The method to the madness," *Newsweek*, October 9, 1999.

27. Webmaster and Tim Brown, http://www.fas.org/nuke/guide/facility/nodung.htm.

28. "Kita Chosen 'Nodon' 200 ki?", *Asahi shimbun*, April 25, 2003.

29. Eya Osamu, quoted in Ota Hiroyuki, "Nodon hassha e no tedate," *Aera*, April 7, 2003, pp. 83–85, at p. 84.

30. Ota Hiroyuki, p. 84.

31. The Brookings Institution, Center for Northeast Asian Policy Studies, 2003 Spring Forum, "Tension on the Peninsula: Korea, Northeast Asia, and the United States," Washington D.C., April 24, 2003.

32. David C. Wright, "Assessment of the N. Korean missile threat," DPRK Briefing Book, Nautilus Institute, March 18, 2003.

33. Richard V. Allen, "Kankoku yo! Kita Chosen no 'tsuyaku' ni naru ka Amerika domei no koku ni naru no ka sentaku seyo," *Sapio*, October 8, 2003, pp. 8–10.

34. *Yomiuri Daily News*, January 11, 2003.

35. Takao Hishinuma, "US, ROK divided on North Korea," Daily Yomiuri Online, January 10, 2003.

36. Don Kirk, "Seoul advises patience on North," *International Herald Tribune*, December 11, 2002.

37. Meredith Woo-Cumings, "South Korean anti-communism," Japan Policy Research Institute (San Diego), Working Paper No. 93, July 2003.

38. "North Korean ties at a crossroads," *Asian Wall St. Journal*, December 16, 2002.

39. "New poll paints U.S. as arrogant superpower," *Japan Times*, June 19, 2003.

40. "North Korean ties at a crossroads," *Asian Wall St. Journal*, December 16, 2002.

41. Takuji Kawata, "Challenge of America—Nukes North's hedge against U.S. attack," Daily Yomiuri Online, January 11, 2003.

42. Anthony Faiola, "Yearning for unification eclipses fear of aggression," *Japan Times*, September 12, 2003.

43. "Korean leader Roh gambles on risky vote of confidence," Agence France-Presse, October 10, 2003.

44. Moon Ihlwan and Brian Bremmer, "The other Korean crisis," *Business Week*, January 20, 2003.

45. Alexandre Y. Mansourov, "Security dilemma, war trap, and the South protectorate over the North," Northeast Asia Peace and Security Network, Special Report, February 10, 2003, http://nautilus.org/for a/security/02138A_Mansourov.html.

## CHAPTER 6

1. Various Japanese media sources, especially editorials in *Asahi* on September 13, 15, and 28, 2003.

2. A survey of 27,000 pupils at Korean schools in Japan found

that just under 20 percent had experienced abuse or assault, with girls and younger boys, those looking least likely to defend themselves, especially affected. (Fujita Yutaka, "Zainichi Korean no kodomotachi ni taisuru iyagarase jittai chosa," *Sekai*, October 2003, pp. 248–254.)

3. For interesting speculation about this, see "Struggle for control of development project," *Weekly Post*, September 23— 29, 2002.

4. "Pyongyang Declaration," September 17, 2002, http://www.mofa.go.jp/region/asia-paci/n_korea/pmv0209/pyongyang.html.

5. See *Hankyoreh Sinmoon*, September 18 and 24, 2002, quoted in Yoon Kooncha, "Sore de mo yappari Nitcho no seijoka wo," Shukan kinyobi, October 18, 2002, p. 10.

6. Wada Haruki, "Can North Korea's Perestroika Succeed?," *Sekai*, November 2002, http://japanfocus.org/005.html.

7. Daily Yomiuri Online, September 30, 2002.

8. Details of the ship and its contents at "Hikiagerareta 'buso kosakusen' daikaibo," Eya Osamu, *Sekai tero senso*, Tokyo, Shogakukan, 2003, pp. 8–9.

9. According to Hwang Jang Yop, the KWP secretary in charge of international affairs who defected to the South in 1997, "Every single mission of every single spy has to be approved by him. So the major terror attacks definitely had his hand in them. This man is a terrorism genius." Kim Hyong Hui, convicted of the 1987 KAL bombing, also insists that orders for the attack came direct from Kim Jong Il and that it was designed to create an atmosphere of terror to spoil the forthcoming Olympic Games in Seoul: *Far Eastern Economic Review*, October 15, 1998.

10. The words of one of the family representatives on NHK television news, October 3, 2002.

11. For the official report into the abductions, and a list of forty suspected additional abductees, see the Asahi site,

http://www.asahi.com/special/abductees/report.html (downloaded June 5, 2003).

12. Korean Institute for National Unification (Seoul), *White Paper on Human Rights in North Korea*, 2001, p. 118.

13. $8 billion was the figure discussed when the LDP's Kanemaru Shin led a multiparty delegation of parliamentarians to Pyongyang in 1990: *Asahi shimbun*, September 16, 2002. Richard Armitage, U.S. Deputy Secretary of State, is said to have told Koizumi that $12 billion would be an appropriate figure when the two met in Tokyo on August 27, 2002: *Weekly Post*, September 9—15, 2002.

14. Quoted from the North Korean media, Ijuin, p. 127.

15. At an electoral meeting, *Mainichi shimbun*, October 14, 2002.

16. Yamazumi Masanori, in *Shukan kinyobi*, September 27, 2002.

17. Announcement by the Chief Cabinet Secretary, October 24, 2002, http://www.mofa.go.jp/region/Asia-paci/n_Korea/ccs0210.html.

18. The two daughters, seventeen and nineteen years old, of Soga Hitomi and her American ex-serviceman husband, Charles Jenkins, were different. They accompanied their mother to the airport when she left for Japan and, with their father, met with Japanese journalists early in 2003.

19. For a detailed account, see Wada Haruki, "Ratchi mondai no kosho o dakai suru michi," in Akashi Yasushi et al, eds., *Do Naru Nitcho kokko kosho*, Sairyusha, 2003, pp. 22–29, at p. 24–5, or "Recovering a Lost Opportunity: Japan–North Korea negotiations in the wake of the Iraq crisis," translated from May 2002 *Sekai* by Mark Caprio, Japan Focus, http://japanfocus.org/036.htm.

20. November 14, 2002, quoted in Wada, "Ratchi mondai." p. 25.

21. *Asahi shimbun*, October 18, 2002.

22. *Asahi shimbun*, October 23, 2002.

23. *Asahi shimbun*, April 16, 2003.

24. NHK Documentary, "Ratchi." September 21, 2003.

25. For a comprehensive list of North Korea books published since 1984, see Wada Haruki and Takasaki Soji, eds., *Kita Chosen hon o do yomu ka*, Akashi shoten, 2003, pp. 198–233.

26. Ota Osamu, "Hi-seiji teki tetsugakusha o yosou omono bomeisha," Wada and Takasaki, eds., pp. 80–91, at p. 91.

27. Park Ryon-Yon, head of the North Korean Foreign Ministry's 4th Bureau, "Ratchi o mitome, keizai kyoryoku hoshiki wo totta no wa 'keizai konnan' ni yoru joho de wa nai," *Shukan kinyobi*, December 13, 2002, pp. 20–21.

28. Such acts tend to occur at times of Korean "crisis," such as the nuclear standoff in 1994, the DPRK's Taepodong missile launch in 1998, and the abduction and nuclear crises of 2002–3.

29. Owaku Masashi and Toyama Toshiki, "Kita Chosen kyoi no shotai," *Aera*, April 14, 2003, pp. 19–21.

30. Okonogi Masao of Keio University, quoted in Owaku and Toyama, p. 20.

31. "Chosen no koi hotondo boryokudan," *Asahi shimbun*, June 14, 2003.

32. International Edition, June 10, 2002.

33. Zalmay Khalilzad et al., "The United States and Asia: toward a New U.S. Strategy and Force Posture" ["The Rand Report"], Washington, 2001, p. 15.

34. Institute for National Strategic Studies, "The United States and Japan: Advancing toward a Mature Partnership," Washington, National Defense University, October 11, 2000, commonly known as the "Armitage Report," http://www.ndu.edu/ndu/sr_japan.html.

35. The National Security Strategy of the United States of America," September 17, 2002, http://www.whitehouse.gov/nsc/nss.pdf.

36. See my "Introduction" to 2nd Revised edition, *The Emptiness of Japanese Affluence*, New York, 2001.

37. Asai Motofumi, "The Bush strategy and Japan's war contingency laws," Japan Focus, posted June 2, 2003,

http://www.zmag.org/content/showarticle.cfm?Section
ID=44&ItemID=3713.

38. For Taniguchi and Takeoka: *Sekai*, July 2002, and *Nihon no shinro*, March 2002.

39. Terashima Jitsuro, "Nazo no sakuhin '1938 nen no tame ni'," *Sekai*, August 2002, and "Japan should not follow U.S. logic of force," *Asahi shimbun*, July 13, 2003.

40. "Ayaui 'seigi' ni keikaishin," *Asahi shimbun*, September 4, 2002.

41. Ida Hiroyuki, "Nihon no 'neocon' no sugao," *Shukan kinyobi*, April 18, 2003, pp. 26–7.

42. Nakanishi together with literary critic Fukuda Kazuya published their "Nuclear Declaration for Japan" in the January 2003 issue of the journal *Voice*.

43. The June 11, 2003 issue of the influential right-wing journal *Sapio* was devoted to the topic "Kim Jong Il no kaku ni wa kaku o" (Handle Kim Jong Il's nuclear weapons with nuclear weapons). An Asahi survey (March 30, 2003) found 43 percent of people taking the view that there was a "danger of war," up 12 points over the previous year, and North Korea is clearly the only danger they have in mind. In September 2002, an international survey on threat perception found a 49-percent perception of threat from North Korea in Japan, as against a 29-percent perception of an Iraq threat in the United States. The Japan figure has almost certainly grown since then (*Asahi shimbun*, September 4, 2002).

44. For Norota and Nishimura, see my "New tunes for an old song: nationalism and Identity in Post-Cold War Japan," in Roy Starrs, ed., *Nations under Siege: Globalization and Nationalism in Asia*, New York and Basingstoke, 2002, pp. 137–168, at p. 151; for Fukuda and Abe: *Sekai*, August 2002, pp. 53–4; for Osawa: *Shukan Kinyobi*, June 7, 2002, p. 8.

**CHAPTER 7**

1. Halliday and Cumings, pp. 128, 163.
2. A. J. Mazarr, *North Korea and the Bomb: A Case Study in Non-proliferation*, London, Palgrave Macmillan, 1995, pp. 16–19.
3. For a description, with photographs, by an American nuclear specialist who visited the site in 1994, see Robert Alvarez, "North Korea: No bygones at Yongbyon," *Bulletin of the Atomic Scientists*, July/August 2003, pp. 39–45.
4. Yi Jong-won, "Chosen hanto datsu reisen e no michi," *Sekai*, November 2003, p. 162.
5. Oberdorfer, p. 261.
6. Yi, pp. 154–172, at p. 160.
7. Yi, p. 160. On the new technologies, Oberdorfer, pp. 270–271.
8. Estimate by General Gary Luck, Commander-in-chief of U.S. forces in Korea at the time. Oberdorfer, p. 324.
9. "Agreed Framework between the DPRK and the US," Geneva, October 21, 1994, http://www.kimsoft.com/2002/geneva-1994.htm.
10. Oberdorfer, p. 336.
11. Oberdorfer, pp. 289–290.
12. William J. Perry, "Review of United States Policy toward North Korea: Findings and Recommendations," October 12, 1999, http://www.state.gov/www/regions/eap/991012_northkorea_rpt.htmls.
13. Selig Harrison, *Korean Endgame: A Strategy for Reunification and U.S. Disengagement*, Princeton and Oxford, Princeton University Press, 2002, pp. 229–230.
14. US Department of State, *Patterns of Global Terrorism 2001*, Washington, Department of State, 2002.
15. Powell to a Senate Foreign Relations Committee hearing, February 5, 2002, http://www.armscontrol.org/factsheets/dprkchron.asp.
16. *The Right Man: The Surprise Presidency of George W. Bush*, New York, Random House, 2003.

17. International Court of Justice, advisory opinion on the legality of the threat or use of nuclear weapons, July 9, 1996, paragraph 97, http://www.mint.gov.my/policy/treaty_nuclear/icj9623_nucthreatopinion.htm.

18. Paul Rogers, "Iran and North Korea: The Next targets?" Open Democracy, October 15, 2003, http://www.opendemocracy.net.

19. Alexandre Mansourov, "The Kelly Process," Nautilus Institute, October 22, 2002, http://www.nautilus.org/fora/security/0206A_Alexandre.html.

20. "From Iraq to North Korea? Hyped Intelligence," *The Oriental Economist*, July 23, 2003.

21. Kamoura Motoaki, "Chosen hanto yuji wa aru no ka," Himuki Fuminori, ed., *Manga de wakatta Kita Chosen mondai*, Tokyo, Maiwei shuppan, 2003, pp. 92–109, at p. 97.

22. "North: Uranium Device Not Used," *Asahi shimbun*, October 29, 2002.

23. Kenneth Quinones, "Beyond collapse, continuity and change in North Korea," unpublished paper, Korean Peninsula Program Director, International Center, Washington, D.C., November 2002.

24. KEDO is totally funded by South Korea and Japan, but headed by an American executive director.

25. Global Security Newswire, October 25, 2002, http://www.nti.org/d_newswire/issues/2002/10/25/4s.html.

26. Yoo Jae-suk, "S. Korean envoys to head north for talks," Associated Press, January 24, 2003.

27. Ann Marie Pecha, "North Korea 11: Pyongyang Never Admitted Nuclear Program, Expert Says," Global Security Newswire, November 15, 2002, http://www.nti.org/d_newswire/issues/2002_11_15.html.

28. Don Oberdorfer, "My private seat at Pyongyang's table," *Washington Post*, November 10, 2002.

29. "S. Korea rift widens over Pyongyang nuclear program," Agence France-Presse, October 25, 2002.

30. Ibid.

31. Richard Armitage, interviewed in *Asahi shimbun*, January 17, 2003. Also Sakijiri Nobuyoshi, "Bei karyoku e tenkan kyocho," *Asahi shimbun*, January 23, 2003.

32. Hartcher and Taylor, cit.

33. Ibid.

34. State of the Union address, January 29, 2003, http://www.whitehouse.gov/news/releases/2003/01/200301 28-19.html.

35. KCNA (Pyongyang), January 28, 2003.

36. Peter Hartcher and Lenore Taylor, "UN engulfed in twin Iraqi and Korean crises," *Australian Financial Review*, February 14, 2003.

37. Colum Lynch, "UN Council stalled in N. Korea," *Washington Post*, April 10, 2003.

38. Joseph Coleman, "Korean nuke issue seen as new flash-point," Associated Press, Seoul, February 11, 2003.

39. Statement by the Korean Anti-Nuke Peace Committee, Pyongyang, January 28, 2003, Nautilus Institute, Special Report, February 7, 2003, http://nautilus.org/pub/ftp/ napsnet/special_reports/KANPC-3critical2.txt.

40. Quoted in "A long bumpy road," editorial, *Asahi shimbun*, April 25, 2003.

41. "Military-first ideology is an ever-victorious banner of our era's cause of independence," Nautilus Institute, Northeast Asia Peace and Security Network, Special Report, April 11, 2003.

42. Quoted in Nicholas D. Kristof, "North Korea's nukes," *International Herald Tribune*, April 30, 2003.

43. Kenneth C. Quinones, "Kita Chosen no kaku kiki—saishu kyokumen de nani ga okiru ka," *Sekai*, April 2003, pp. 119–133, at p. 122.

44. Takao Hishinuma, "US, ROK divided on North Korea," Daily Yomiuri Online, January 10, 2003.

45. Desaix Anderson, "Crisis and North Korea: The US Strategic

Future in East Asia." Nautilus Institute, Policy Planning Online, March 27, 2003.

46. James Lilley, former U.S. ambassador to South Korea, stresses this China role; see interview in *Nihon keizai shimbun*, July 27, 2003.

47. *Asahi shimbun*, April 29, 2003.

48. As compiled by *Yomiuri shimbun* from diplomatic sources, "Kita no 'mikatte' 4 dankai," *Yomiuri shimbun*, June 27, 2003. See also "Kita Chosen, 'fukashin yakosuku' o," *Asahi shimbun*, April 29, 2003.

49. Steven R. Weisman, "U.S. scoffs at latest offer from North Korea," *International Herald Tribune*, April 30, 2003.

50. Howard H. Baker, interview, daily Yomiuri Online, May 5, 2003.

51. Kita Chosen shuzaihan, " 'Kakuheiki hoyu' no shogeki," *Aera*, May 12, 2003, pp. 8–10.

52. David Wall, "Kelly's 'fairies' threaten peace," *Japan Times*, May 1, 2003; see also Gregory Elich, "The Nuclear Frame-up of North Korea", Centre for Research on Globalization, July 4, 2003, http://www.globalresearch.ca/articles/EL1307A.html.

53. *Asahi shimbun*, April 26, 2003.

54. Jonathan Pollack, "The United States, North Korea, and the end of the 'Agreed Framework'," *Naval War College Review*, Summer 2003, vol. LVI, No. 3, http://yaleglobal.yale.edu/about/pdfs/USnorthKorea.pdf.

55. Christopher Torchia, "South Korea's Prime Minister does not believe the north has nukes," Associated Press, Seoul, February 11, 2003; Jae-Yun Shim, "Roh not sure of North Korea's nuke possession," *Korea Times*, June 2, 2003.

56. David E. Sanger, "U.S. fears warhead gains by Pyongyang," *Sydney Morning Herald*, July 2, 2003.

57. Julian Borger and Jonathan Watts, "North Korea offers to lift nuclear threat," *Guardian Weekly*, May 1–7, 2003.

58. Curt Weldon, "A North Korea Peace Initiative," Foreign Policy Research Institute, June 26, 2003, http://www.fpri.org.

59. *Asahi shimbun*, June 4, 2003.

60. BBC Monitoring, Seoul, October 21, 2003.

61. "Talking it out in Korea," editorial, *Boston Globe*, June 15, 2003.

62. William J. Perry, "It's either nukes or negotiation," ed., *Washington Post*, July 23, 2003.

63. Quoted in Thomas E. Ricks and Glenn Kessler, "U.S., N. Korea drifting toward war, warns Perry," *Washington Post*, July 14, 2003.

64. Marian Wilkinson, "US prepares to open door to flood of North Korean refugees," *Sydney Morning Herald*, July 30, 2003.

65. Martin Chulov and Cameron Stewart, "North Korean scientists defect," *Weekend Australian*, April 19–20.

66. C. Kenneth Quinones, "The North Korea Nuclear Crisis: Contingency Planning for the 'End Game'," Unpublished Paper, International Center, Washington, January 6, 2003.

67. Chulov and Stewart, cit.

68. "From Iraq to North Korea: Hyped intelligence," *The Oriental Economist*, July 23, 2003.

69. On "Operations Plan 5030," see Bruce B. Auster and Kevin Whitelaw, "Upping the ante for Kim Jong Il," *U.S. News and World Report*, July 21, 2003.

70. Australian Department of Foreign Affairs and Trade, "Proliferation Security Initiative, Brisbane Meeting, July 9–10, 2003." Countries involved: Australia, France, Germany, Italy, Japan, the Netherlands, Poland, Portugal, Spain, the UK, and the United States, http://www.dfat.gov.au/globalissues/psi/.

71. The *Sosan*, a North Korean cargo ship carrying a perfectly legal consignment of Scud missiles bound for Yemen, was boarded and briefly detained by the Spanish Navy, at U.S. request, in December 2002, 600 miles off the horn of Africa.

72. Seymour Hersh, "The Cold Test—What the administration knew about Pakistan and the North Korean nuclear program,"

*The New Yorker*, January 20, 2003, http://www.newyorker.com
/printable/?fact/030127fa_fact.

73. "Top US official slams North Korea, demands end to nuclear
    drive," *Agence France-Presse*, July 31, 2003.

74. Michael E. O'Hanlon, Susan E. Rice, and James B. Steinberg,
    "The New National Security Strategy and Preemption,"
    Policy Brief No. 113, Brookings Institution, July 2003,
    http://www.brookings.edu/comm/policybriefs/pb113.htm.

75. "Peace Process: Japan push for U.S. to heed North Korea's
    8–point plan," *Asahi shimbun*, June 13, 2003.

76. Masaru Honda, "Japan must have its own scenario on North
    Korea," *Asahi shimbun*, June 13, 2003.

77. "Tokyo eyes no-war pledge, aid," *Asahi shimbun*, August 15,
    2003.

78. On the Beijing-Pyingyang communications, see "Hu Jintao
    writes to Kim Jong-il to open door to six-party talks," *Hong
    Kong Economic Journal*, September 5, 2003, reproduced in
    http://www.nautilus.org/pub/ftp/napsnet/special_reports/H
    uJinTao-Letter.txt.

79. "DPRK Puts Forward 'Package of Solutions' to Nuclear Crisis,"
    Korean Central News Agency, August 29, 2003, reproduced in
    Nautilus Institute, Northeast Asia Peace and Security Net-
    work, Special Report, September 5, 2003, http://www.nau-
    tilus.org/pub/ftp/napsnet/special_reports/DPRK-Package
    Solution.txt.

80. "Dokyumento gekido no Nanboku Chosen—Rokusha
    kyogi no seika to wa?" Sekai, November 2003, pp.
    165–172, at p. 169.

81. "South Korea, Russia wants diplomatic push, China blames
    US Policy," *Agence France-Presse*, September, 1 2003.

82. ExxonMobil is said to be aggressively lobbying the Bush
    administration on this project, which would require a $500
    million–$4 billion investment over four years, and Repub-
    lican Congressman Kurt Weldon was due to be received by

both Kim Jong Il in Pyongyang and Roh Moo Hyun in Seoul on an October 2003 visit designed to promote it. (Kwon Sun Taek, "US seeking to provide Sakhalin natural gas to North Korea," *Donga Ilbo*, September 29, 2003.)

83. Alexandre Mansourov, "The North Koreans have come to the nuclear Rubicon now," Nautilus Institute, April 23, 2003.

84. Tetsuya Hakoda, "North Korea plays wild card," *Asahi shimbun*, October 19, 2002.

85. Mansourov, "The Kelly Process," p. 3. See also Andrew Mack, "North Korea's Latest Nuclear Gambit," Nautilus Institute, Special Report, 21 October 2002.

86. "Endgame in Korea," *The Nation*, November 18, 2002.

## CHAPTER 8

1. Maurice Strong, special adviser to UN Secretary General. Kofi Annan, quoted in Tracy McVeigh, "North Korea and the US on a slide towards conflict," *The Observer*, April 6, 2003.

2. R. James Woolsey (CIA director between 1993 and 1995) and Thomas G. McInerney (retired three-star Air Force lieutenant general and former assistant vice chief of staff), "The next Korean War," *The Wall Street Journal*, August 5, 2003.

3. Ishikura Ayako, "Senzen omowaseru, Kita Chosen no seikatsu," "Koe," *Asahi shimbun* (Nagoya), January 23, 2003.

4. Cited in C. Kenneth Quinones, "Dualism in the Bush Administration's North Korea policy," February 2003, unpublished article ("for *Asian Perspective*"), International Center, Washington.

5. Xu Wenji, professor of the North-East Asia Research Institute in the Jilin provincial capital Changchun, quoted in Hamish McDonald, "The rogue next door," *Sydney Morning Herald*, February 22, 2003.

6. In the Gulf War of 1991 300 tons of DU were used, and in the Afghanistan war an estimated 700 tons. North Korea's deeply embedded facilities would almost certainly attract a high use of D.U.-type weapons.

7. Haruki Wada, "East Asia and the Cold War: Reinterpreting its meaning in the new millennium," Chung-in Moon, Odd Arne Westad and Gyoo-hyoung Kahng, eds., *Ending the Cold War in Korea: Theoretical and Historical Perspectives*, Seoul, Yonsei University, 2001, pp. 69–88. See also Wada's "The Era of Northeast Asia," *Hangyoreh shinmoon*, Seoul, March 10, 2003, English translation in "Japan Focus," http://www.japanfocus.org, and his *Tohoku Ajia kyodo no ie*, Heibonsha, 2003; also Kan Sanjon, *Tohoku Ajia kyodo no ie o mezashite*, Heibonsha, 2001.

8. "Asia Cooperation Dialogue," Chiang Mai, June 21, 2003. See also Tanaka Sakai, "Shizuka ni naru Ajia no togo," Tanaka Sakai no kokusai nyusu kaisetsu, July 18, 2003, http://tanakanews.com.

9. Yi Jong-won, " 'Hokuto Ajia-ken' tenbo hirake," *Asahi shimbun*, June 4, 2003.

10. Roh Moo-Hyun, lecture to Tsinghua University, Beijing, July 9, 2003.